the Wilds

REJOICE IN THE LORD ALWAY: AND AGAIN I SAY, REJOICE.

PHILIPPIANS 4:4

PHILIPPIANS

THE SECRET OF OUTRAGEOUS, CONTAGIOUS JOY!

A SIX-WEEK BIBLE STUDY BY
RAND HUMMEL

Other Titles by Rand Hummel

- A Lasting Impression Series for Juniors
  God is...
  What Does God Say About My Sin?
- Colossians: Jesus Christ—The Visible Icon of the Invisible God
- Daniel—Living with Lion Like Character
- Five Smooth Stones Scripture Memory Plan
- God & I Time Treasures: Volumes 1, 2, and 3
- James: A Guidebook to Spiritual Maturity
- Jonah's Magnificent God
- Joseph: A Man with Character
- New Testament Postcards
- 1 Peter: Living in the Face of Ridicule
- 2 Peter: Exposing Counterfeit Christianity
- Philippians: Outrageous, Contagious Joy
- Rightside Up Attitude in an Upside Down World
- 2 Timothy—Character in Crisis
- Titus: Living a God-Centered Life in a Self-Centered World
- The Wonderful Works of God Series for Juniors
  Daniel, Jonah, Joseph, and Joshua

All Scripture is quoted from the Authorized King James Version.

Philippians—The Secret of Outrageous, Contagious Joy!
A Six-week Bible Study
By Rand Hummel
Cover design by Craig Stouffer

© 2016, 2007, 2004, 2003 The Wilds Christian Association, Inc.
PO Box 509
Taylors, SC 29687
Phone: (864) 268-4760
Fax: (864) 292-0743

Printed in the United States of America. All rights reserved. No part of this publication may be reproduced or transmitted in any form or by any means, electronic or mechanical, including photocopying, recording, or any data storage/retrieval system, without written permission from the publisher.

ISBN: 978-0-9861075-3-5

PHILIPPIANS

The Secret of Outrageous, Contagious Joy!

"Rejoice in the Lord alway: and again I say, Rejoice."
Philippians 4:4

FOUR LIFE-CHANGING, JOY-PRODUCING PRINCIPLES

Principle One:
A God-confidence produces sustaining joy!
Philippians 1:1-30

Week One: A God-confidence gives me a thankful heart.
(Philippians 1:1-11)
- Thank God by serving (1:1-2)
- Thank God by praying (1:3-4)
- Thank God by believing (1:5-6)
- Thank God by loving (1:7-8)
- Thank God by growing (1:9-11)

Week Two: A God-confidence gives me a trusting heart.
(Philippians 1:12-30)
- Trust God in the face of difficulties (1:12-14)
- Trust God in the face of dissension (1:15-18)
- Trust God in the face of death (1:18b-21)
- Trust God in the face of dilemma (1:21-26)
- Trust God in the face of disagreement (1:27-30)

Principle Two:
An unselfish spirit produces unspeakable joy!
Philippians 2:1-30

Week Three: The attitude of an unselfish Christ.
(Philippians 2:1-11)
- The heart of an unselfish Christ (2:1-2)
- The motivation of an unselfish Christ (2:3-4)
- The mind of an unselfish Christ (2:5-6)
- The humility of an unselfish Christ (2:7-8)
- The glory of an unselfish Christ (2:9-11)

Week Four: The attitude of an unselfish Christian.
(Philippians 2:12-30)
- The unselfish attitude of an obedient believer (2:12-13)
- The unselfish attitude of a blameless child (2:14-15)
- The unselfish attitude of a joyful servant (2:15b-18)
- The unselfish attitude of a sincere friend: Timothy (2:19-24)
- The unselfish attitude of a selfless servant: Epaphroditus (2:25-30)

Principle Three:
An eternal focus produces outrageous joy!
Philippians 3:1-21
Week Five: An eternal focus.
(Philippians 3:1-21)
- Never focus on your past accomplishments – Part 1 (3:1-6)
- Never focus on your past accomplishments – Part 2 (3:7-11)
- Never focus on your present accomplishments (3:12-16)
- Focus on the accomplishments of Christlike leaders (3:17-19)
- Focus on the eternal accomplishments of Christ (3:20-21)

Principle Four:
A contented heart produces contagious joy!
Philippians 4:1-23
Week Six: A contented heart.
(Philippians 4:1-23)
- Contentment comes from an understanding of God's people (4:1-3)
- Contentment comes from an understanding of God's presence (4:4-6)
- Contentment comes from an understanding of God's peace (4:7-9)
- Contentment comes from an understanding of God's power (4:10-13)
- Contentment comes from an understanding of God's provision (4:14-23)

Dear Bible study friend,

Philippians is about JOY! Smiles! Laughter! Do you remember what it was like when you were just a little kid? You didn't care what you looked like, what you smelled like, or if the boys (if you're a girl) or if the girls (if you're a boy) even knew you existed. You were a happy kid. You did not fear bad grades, family problems, or Middle East war. You were happy! You smiled! What is it about growing older that makes smiles disappear? Why does laughter often leave when the grown-up years come?

Paul had four life-motivating, joy-producing, smile-inducing principles going for him. Paul's joy was both outrageous (few could understand it) and contagious (many caught it)! And guess what? We can have that same kind of joy! For the next six weeks we will examine each one of Paul's joy-producing principles in depth. Get ready to study. Get ready to learn. Get ready to smile.

Keep smiling,

Rand

Rand Hummel

Principle One:

A God-confidence produces sustaining joy!

Philippians 1:1-30

Week 1: A God-confidence gives me a thankful heart.
Monday: Philippians 1:1-2

Thank God by Serving

Paul and Timotheus, the servants of Jesus Christ, to all the saints in Christ Jesus which are at Philippi, with the bishops and deacons: grace be unto you, and peace, from God our Father, and from the Lord Jesus Christ.

There are two kinds of people—those who choose to be joyful and those who do not. Paul offered his friends in Philippi the secrets of joy. If he, confined in his frustrating and often irritating situation, could be joyful, so could his friends. Philippians is about JOY! Smiles! Laughter! When Paul thought of the Corinthians, he remembered a group of struggling believers. When Paul wrote the Thessalonians, he thought of their hope of the Lord's return. When Paul penned a letter to the Galatians, he focused on those who needed a clearer understanding of the law. When Paul thought of his young believing friends in Philippi, he got a smile on his face.

1. Paul's letter to the Philippians is all about joy. Two joyful servants wrote to a group of joyful believers about the joy that they both had from the Lord Jesus Christ. Today we sign off our letters and e-mails at the end. In Paul's day they signed on at the beginning so the recipients knew who the letter was from. Paul and Timothy called themselves **servants**. They were not big shots. They did not view themselves as powerful leaders. They were just two bondslaves excited about serving the Lord. An honest appraisal of our own abilities, gifts, and influence keeps us from being self-confident. We have nothing to offer apart from what God has given us! Paul and Timothy were simply dedicated servants. On a regular basis, whom do you serve? How do you serve them? How often do you serve them? Who would serve them if you quit serving them? Why do you serve them? Your answers to these five questions reveal how well you are doing as a **servant** of God.

_____

_____

2. These two servants were serving God by serving the **saints** of Philippi. Most of these **saints** we do not know. But a few of them can be studied through some private investigative work in Acts 16. According to Acts 16:16-34, what do you know about the saint who by occupation was a Philippian jailor? What turned his attention to God? What happened to his entire family?

_____

_____

What do you know about Saint Lydia? What did she do for a living and what was she doing when Paul first found her? Read Acts 16:12-15 and give an investigative report about this Philippian saint.

_____

_____

(Note: What do you think the phrase **where prayer was wont to be made** in Acts 16:13 is talking about? Saints are expected to pray. Children should be able to catch their parents praying each morning. Parents should be able to catch their children praying each night. All Christian "saints" should be able to catch each other praying through life's struggles. When and where could someone "catch" you praying?)

_____

3. These **saints** had some friends. In their little group of believers, there were some caring friends who rose to leadership as they helped and encouraged spiritual growth among the saints. These friends are called **bishops and deacons**. The **bishops** could also be called overseers, elders, pastors, and pastor-teachers. Your pastor is your friend. Those men in your church who have shown the qualifications of a mature believer are often chosen to be **deacons** and elders. These local church leaders are on your side. They are there for you. If your joy is slipping away because of some difficulty at home or disappointment in life, which spiritual leader would you go to in your church and why?

_____

_____

_____

4. **Philippi.** Most cities have a unique reputation and Philippi is no exception. This ancient city was almost non-existent before it was refounded by Philip II (the father of Alexander the Great). Around 31 B.C. Philippi was heavily settled by retired Roman soldiers who were incredibly loyal to Caesar. Christians were targeted for persecution because of their refusal to join in with this "Caesar" worship. It is amazing that in the midst of persecution, suffering, misunderstanding, and animosity the Philippian believers are still remembered for their joy. What difficulty are you presently facing that keeps you from rejoicing in the Lord always? In what way do you have it tougher than those early believers in Philippi? What is hindering your joy?

_____

_____

_____

5. Salutations! **Grace be unto you, and peace, from God our Father, and from the Lord Jesus Christ.** Paul made it a matter of emphasis to start many of his letters to young believers with the same life-changing, security-building truths. This same greeting is found in Romans 1:7, 1 Corinthians 1:3, 2 Corinthians 1:2, Ephesians 1:2, Colossians 1:2-3, and 2 Thessalonians 1:2. It is almost as if Paul wanted every individual who received his letters to understand the importance of God's grace from above, God's peace from within, and how they are intrinsically linked to our relationship with our Lord Jesus Christ. Describe the time in your life when you accepted God's undeserved **grace** by receiving the forgiveness of your sins and were overwhelmed with the **peace** that only saving faith in the Lord Jesus Christ can bring.

_____

_____

_____

Paul's God-confidence gave him a thankful heart as seen in the way he served. He could fervently serve with joy as he trusted God's power and providence. We can also serve with outrageous, contagious joy as we learn to live each day with such God-confidence.

Week 1: A God-confidence gives me a thankful heart.
Tuesday: Philippians 1:3-4

Thank God by praying

I thank my God upon every remembrance of you, always in every prayer of mine for you all making request with joy.

1. **I thank my God.** Paul was a thankful guy. He didn't just "think" about his friends in Rome, Corinth, Thessalonica, and Philippi, he "thanked" God for them. Although some of the people he thanked God for brought him great joy, there were others who brought him intense grief. He thanked God for them too. True, heartfelt "thanks" speaks volumes. You cannot really "thank God" without recognizing that the things that have already happened in your life (both the good and the bad) were for your best. Thanking God for what He has already done in the past reveals a confidence in Him and in His sovereign will. Is there anyone or anything in your life that you have a hard time thanking God for? Is there anyone or anything that you refuse to thank God for? In what way do you feel that has God been unfair to you?

_____
_____
_____

2. I like the way Paul keeps his relationship with God on a personal level. He did not just say, "I thank God," but, "I thank **my** God." In both the first and last chapters of this book Paul uses the words "my God." Religious people can talk about "the God" of their religion. Even moralistic unbelievers can refer to "the God" in heaven. But only true, born-again believers who have repented of their sins and trusted Christ alone for their eternal salvation can say "my God." How often do you personally refer to God as "my God" in your conversations with your friends? Describe when "the God" of the universe became "your God" in salvation.

_____
_____
_____

3. **I thank my God upon every remembrance of you.** Saying "thank you" is not just a polite statement, it is a verbal recognition that someone has had an impact on your life. Not only did God use Paul to impact the young believers in Philippi, God used the Philippian believers to impact Paul. Every time Paul thought of them, he thanked God for them. Every time he thought of the jailor listening in on his and Silas' prison concert, he thanked God. Every time he remembered Lydia and the others meeting at the river to pray and give praise to God, Paul's heart was filled with thanksgiving. Why? Philippians 1:5 (which we will study tomorrow) gives the answer. Paul thanked God for those who heard the truth of the gospel and accepted it. He thanked God for those who chose to trust God and continued to live for Him. He was thankful to God for the work He did in their lives and thankful for the Philippians who accepted God's calling. What believers can you thank God for? Who have you encouraged to be saved? If you have never experienced this joy, keep praying and sharing your faith so that someday you will. List a few names of some individuals God has brought into your life whom you would love to see saved.

_____
_____

4. **Always in every prayer of mine for you all.** Unlike Paul, we must be careful when using 100% words such as **always** and **every**. Our inconsistencies undermine our abilities to live up to **always** and **every**. Don't you wish you could say that you **always** pray **every** day? Don't you wish you would **always** obey **every** time? Most of us can't say that. Instead of being "always-every" Christians, we often live like "sometimes-maybe" Christians. Paul was so consumed with his God and his friends that **every** time he prayed he **always** thanked God for them. Such consistency in Paul's life is seen in many of his New Testament letters. He told the Roman Christians, **without ceasing I make mention of you always in my prayers** (Romans 1:9); he encouraged his Christian friends in Corinth by saying, **I thank my God always on your behalf** (1 Corinthians 1:4); to the Ephesians he testified that he was **giving thanks always for all things unto God and the Father** (Ephesians 5:20); and to the Thessalonian believers he said **we pray always for you, that our God would count you worthy of this calling, and fulfil all the good pleasure of His goodness** (2 Thessalonians 1:11). Paul was an "always-every" man. His consistency is convicting. List three areas in your life that you would love to change from a "sometimes-maybe" to an "always-every" type person.

_____

_____

_____

5. **Making request with joy.** You need never to be afraid to pray about anything when you are praying with the right heart attitude. When your motives are pure before God, never fear asking Him for anything. Paul's thankful and trusting heart enabled him to make **request with joy** knowing that God, in His wisdom and sovereignty, would do what was best for His glory and the good of those Paul was praying for. Most Wednesday night prayer meetings in our local churches take time for prayer "requests" that are heavy on the hearts of individuals. You can learn much about someone when you ask them for their most important prayer request. List your two most important prayer requests and compare them with the prayer requests Paul prayed to God for his friends. What is the difference between yours and Paul's?

Your first request: _____

Your second request: _____

Paul's request in Romans 1:9-12

_____

_____

Paul's request in Philippians 1:9-11

_____

_____

*Paul's God-confidence gave him a thankful heart as seen in the way he served and the way he prayed. He could honestly and eagerly pray with **joy** as he trusted God's goodness and greatness. We can also pray with outrageous, contagious joy as we learn to live each day with such a God-confidence. "Lord, help us to be confident in You."*

Week 1: A God-confidence gives me a thankful heart.
Wednesday: Philippians 1:5-6

Thank God by believing

For your fellowship in the gospel from the first day until now; being confident of this very thing, that He which hath begun a good work in you will perform it until the day of Jesus Christ.

1. We learned yesterday of Paul's thankful heart and how he was especially thankful for the open reception the Philippians had for the gospel. When Paul thanked God for their **fellowship in the gospel** he was thanking God for the way his Philippian friends participated, accepted, and believed in the death, burial, and resurrection of Jesus Christ. In a world that is consumed with rejecting the truth, we should be just as thankful as Paul when our friends accept and believe the gospel. The Philippian believers obviously had a consistency and a commitment or Paul would not have said **from the first day until now**. These people trusted the gospel and stuck with it. The word **fellowship** (*koinonia*) has the idea of "sharing" with others. These believers were giving, sharing, fellowshipping people. They shared their money with Paul for the spread of the gospel; they shared their faith and love as they encouraged each other; they shared in their praise and worship of God as they met in various homes. It is the sharing of your time, your money, and your heart that brings you to a closer relationship with others. Most of our churches have fellowship halls, fellowship dinners, and fellowship hours, but true heart-knitting, soul-searching, God-seeking times of fellowship are not as common. How has Christian fellowship encouraged your walk with God in the last year and how have you encouraged someone else in a similar way?

_____

_____

_____

2. **Being confident of this very thing.** Paul loved the word **confident**. Paul loved the joy of living with confidence. It is amazing how total confidence in God's wisdom, confidence in God's power, and confidence in God's sovereignty can replace the frown on your heart with a smile on your face. I am confident, assured, fully persuaded, convinced, certain, positive, and have no doubt that God has everything under control. He is God!!! What makes us so confident in ourselves? Admit it. We are certainly not as smart or as wise as God; we definitely are not as strong or as powerful as God; we could never keep things under control like God does…so why are we so self-confident and so sure of ourselves? David said in Psalm 118:8, **It is better to trust in the LORD than to put confidence in man** (that includes yourself). Solomon tells us in Proverbs 3:26, **For the LORD shall be thy confidence, and shall keep thy foot from being taken.** How can you use these two verses to encourage one of your fearful friends to trust God and be confident in His power?

_____

_____

3. Six times in the book of Philippians Paul uses the word *peitho* or confidence. Five times each in Romans, Galatians, and Hebrews, and eight other times in the epistles…that is twenty-nine times in seven letters that Paul refers to confidence. Self-confidence will get us nowhere. God-confidence sets you up to live a life of joy. Meditate on the following verses and write a short application of how a God-confidence continues to encourage your heart.

Philippians 1:6 **Being confident of this very thing, that He which hath begun a good work in you will perform it until the day of Jesus Christ.**

Philippians 1:14 **And many of the brethren in the Lord, waxing confident by my bonds, are much more bold to speak the word without fear.**

Philippians 1:25 **And having this confidence, I know that I shall abide and continue with you all for your furtherance and joy of faith.**

Philippians 2:24 **But I trust** (am confident) **in the Lord that I also myself shall come shortly.**

Philippians 3:3-4 **For we are the circumcision, which worship God in the spirit, and rejoice in Christ Jesus, and have no confidence in the flesh. Though I might also have confidence in the flesh. If any other man thinketh that he hath whereof he might trust in the flesh, I more.**

---

4. **He which hath begun a good work in you will perform it until the day of Jesus Christ.** The word **He** in this verse is speaking of God—all powerful, almighty, omnipotent God. The words **begun** and **perform** are the bookends of your salvation experience. God started (**hath begun**) your salvation and He will complete (**perform** or perfect) it. Have you ever doubted your salvation? Have you ever prayed one of those "just-in-case" prayers? Counseling those who doubt their salvation reveals an interesting truth. Normally, where we look for our assurance of salvation is where we looked for our salvation. Do you live with a self-confidence or a God-confidence?

THE SELF-CONFIDENCE APPROACH TO DOUBTS

If we constantly focus on self ("Did I pray it right? Did I have enough faith? Did I say the right words? Did I really, really, really believe like I should have?"), we will constantly struggle with assurance of salvation. The focus in that kind of thinking is on "I" and not on God. We cannot earn favor with God or be good enough to be saved, so why do we think our eternal security is based on how "I" believed or how good "I" am?

THE GOD-CONFIDENCE APPROACH TO DOUBTS

Those who looked to God and God alone for their salvation attack doubts in a different way. "Lord, You are the one that convicted me. You are the one who promised to forgive me. You are the one who drew me to Yourself. Therefore, You are the only one who can keep my salvation for me. Lord, I trust You and You alone with my eternal destiny."

Describe how you have dealt with doubts in the past and see how it lines up with the two approaches explained above.

"Lord, I am confident, I am persuaded, I am sure, I have no doubts that You will keep me in Your hands where nothing can remove me from Your eternal protection. Thank you, Lord."

Week 1: A God-confidence gives me a thankful heart.
Thursday: Philippians 1:7-8

Thank God by loving

Even as it is meet for me to think this of you all, because I have you in my heart; inasmuch as both in my bonds, and in the defence and confirmation of the gospel, ye all are partakers of my grace. For God is my record, how greatly I long after you all in the bowels of Jesus Christ.

1. We are never more Godlike (and joyful) than when we love others.

Beloved, let us love one another: for love is of God; and every one that loveth is born of God, and knoweth God. He that loveth not knoweth not God; for God is love (1 John 4:7-8). We can thank God for loving us by modeling His love toward others. In a world of hate, godly love can break through the hardest of hearts. Through his own example, Paul taught the Philippians six very important principles about godly love that he explains in Philippians 1:7-8. Slowly read those verses again thinking of these truths.

- Godly love involves right choices that result in right feelings.
- Godly love comes from the heart and is not hypocritical, fake, or phony.
- Godly love does not run or hide during the difficult times of life.
- Godly love is a natural overflow of God's grace toward us.
- Godly love never goes unnoticed by God Himself.
- Godly love loves others in the same way that my Lord Jesus Christ loves me.

2. Godly love involves right choices that result in right feelings.

The words **it is meet for me to think this of you all** simply means "it is only right for me to feel this way about all of you." Even though love is a command and a choice, it does involve feelings and emotions. We must be careful not to get out of balance in this by either basing decisions solely on emotional feelings or by suffocating the feelings to the point of squeezing all joy out of love. Have you ever been in love? Try to explain how it felt.

_____

_____

3. Godly love comes from the heart and is not hypocritical, fake, or phony.

Paul assured his friends saying, **I have you in my heart.** Nothing is more repulsive than someone "pretending" that they are in love with all the soupy, syrupy silliness that accompanies fake love. Some junior high girls will "fake love" to get acceptance or popularity. Some teen guys will "fake love" to satisfy their egos or their lust. Some "fake love" to manipulate others to get what they want. Godly love that comes from the heart is real, is focused on others, and will last a lifetime. Pick out two phrases from Romans 12:9-10 and explain what Paul is saying about true love and how it views others.

_____

_____

4. **GODLY LOVE DOES NOT RUN OR HIDE DURING THE DIFFICULT TIMES OF LIFE.**

The Philippian believers stuck with Paul even when he was **in bonds** (thrown in prison for preaching the gospel). They were not ashamed to be identified with both Paul and the gospel. It is sad to say that the fear of rejection, the fear of what others will say, and the fear of being different causes many professing believers to run and hide instead of living for God. Do you fear rejection? Do you fear taking a stand for God? Read 1 John 4:18 and explain the contrast between love and fear.

_____

_____

_____

5. **GODLY LOVE IS A NATURAL OVERFLOW OF GOD'S GRACE TOWARD US.**

Paul told the Philippians that they were **partakers of grace** with him. He could not have survived his imprisonment and persecution without God's grace. It would have been easy for Paul to have become angry and bitter against his persecuting God-haters. He refused by accepting God's grace. Read Hebrews 12:15 and explain the result of refusing to accept (failing) the grace of God.

_____

_____

6. **GODLY LOVE NEVER GOES UNNOTICED BY GOD HIMSELF.**

God is my record. God is my witness. God knows my heart! You can fool your friends, but you cannot fool God. He knows your heart! You can fool your family members, but you cannot fool God. He knows your thoughts! In essence Paul was saying, "If any of you think that I do not mean it when I say I love you just like Christ loves me, I call God Himself to the witness stand. He knows my heart. I go on record saying that God will testify that what I am saying is true. I long after you. I desire to be with you. God is my witness." Read Matthew 6:4, 6, and 18 and explain how what we do for God will never go unnoticed.

_____

_____

7. **GODLY LOVE LOVES OTHERS IN THE SAME WAY THAT MY LORD JESUS CHRIST LOVES ME.**

For God is my record, how greatly I long after you all in the bowels of Jesus Christ. We don't use the phrase **in the bowels** today like it was used when the English Bible was first written. Instead of saying **in the bowels** (referring to the innermost, deepest seat of emotion), we would say "from the bottom of my heart." However you say it, the affection that Paul had for his friends in Philippi causes any love we have for our friends to pale in comparison. Most of us are too busy loving ourselves to love others. Godly care that seeks the best for others is a true hallmark of a godly Christian. How did Jesus Christ love me? Talk about total sacrifice! He left heaven for me. He became a man for me. He was mocked for me. He was beaten for me. His beard was yanked out by the handfuls for me. His back was bloodied for me. His hands and feet were pierced for me. He died for me. He did all this in order to bring me to God. Jesus Christ loved me that much. My love for others is seen by my commitment to bring them closer to God. Do you share Christ with your friends? Have you ever suffered any ridicule or rejection for telling someone about Christ's love? Paul loved others like Christ loved him. We all should do the same.

"Lord, help me to love others like Paul loved the Philippians. Help me to love others like You loved me. Help me to stop loving myself long enough to start loving others. Help me, Lord."

Week 1: A God-confidence gives me a thankful heart.
Friday: Philippians 1:9-11

Thank God by growing

And this I pray, that your love may abound yet more and more in knowledge and in all judgment; that ye may approve things that are excellent; that ye may be sincere and without offence till the day of Christ; being filled with the fruits of righteousness, which are by Jesus Christ, unto the glory and praise of God.

1. Paul gives us his personal prayer list for his friends. He did not pray for their physical health or numeric growth but he asked God to help them **abound** spiritually (grow) in five areas: love, excellence, integrity, fruitful life, and glorifying God. Would you be willing to commit a few minutes a day to pray these same five requests for your closest friends? List their first names and begin praying for them right now.

_____

_____

_____

2. **Love**

You don't have to study the New Testament long before you see an emphasis on love: love for God, love from God, and love for others. Paul did not say that the Philippians did not love, but that there was room for growth in their love. He prayed that their love would **abound**. This word has the idea of overflowing from excess or something left over (see, leftovers are not always bad). As we spend time in God's Word, our hearts will naturally be filled to overflowing with His love, patience, and kindness. Paul prayed specifically that their **love** would spill over in two areas: **in knowledge and in all judgment**. True **knowledge** is the kind that is both learned and experienced from obedience to the truth. Peter said it well when he said, **seeing ye have purified your souls in obeying the truth through the Spirit unto unfeigned love of the brethren, see that ye love one another with a pure heart fervently** (1 Peter 1:22). Discernment (**judgment**) is the practical application of such knowledge. **Love** that is discerning and knowledgeable knows what to do and why it is doing it. Briefly explain how your love for God and others has grown in direct correlation to your growth in your personal Bible study and meditation.

_____

_____

3. **Excellence**

There is an interesting progression in these verses. Your discerning, knowledgeable love helps you to approve what is excellent (discern what is best). We should never be satisfied with the ordinary or content with the mundane. There are many good churches, good schools, and good Christians, but there are not so many excellent churches, schools, and Christians. Good could be the enemy of excellent. Your love for others should drive you to want the very best for them. The difference between good and excellent is found in a little extra time, a little extra thought, and a little extra sacrifice. How can an anti-ordinary, anti-apathetic, anti-mundane love for God impact what you do each day?

_____

_____

4. Integrity

If God somehow chose you as an illustration and put your public and private life on the big screen for all to see, would you be embarrassed? Is what your family and friends observe each day the real you? Do you have a secret life that no one knows about? Paul prayed that the Philippians would be **sincere and without offence** (pure and blameless) which deals with issues others cannot see. The word **sincere** has the idea of being put under a spotlight where every minute detail can be examined. The phrase **without offence** gives the idea of being blameless or not having any hidden secret that would cause someone to doubt your love for God. Your knowledgeable love for God that helps you discern what is excellent also motivates you to choose a pure, blameless lifestyle that is lived from the inside out. We need to daily ask for God's protection to help us live a life of integrity in this wicked world. Write out a short prayer that you could repeatedly pray each day asking God to keep you pure, blameless, sincere, and without offence.

_____
_____
_____

5. Fruitful life

Our progression continues. Knowledgeable love results in excellent discernment which motivates internal integrity which feeds external righteousness. Sounds heavy but it is really not. You do right because you are right because you think right because you love right. Right? When Paul prayed that his Philippian friends would be **filled with the fruits of righteousness** he was trusting that the right seeds had already been planted in their hearts. The seeds of godly love, spiritual excellence, and internal integrity will result in a life filled to overflowing with love, joy, peace, patience, kindness, goodness, faithfulness, gentleness, and self-control. Do you know where this list came from? To his believing friends in Galatia, Paul called these characteristics **fruit of the Spirit**. The phrase **of the Spirit** coincides with the phrase we are studying today, **which are by Jesus Christ.** We cannot live a fruitful life on our own, but only by Jesus Christ through His Holy Spirit. With this in mind, read Philippians 2:13 and explain how God by His Spirit could help you to be more loving, more patient, or more faithful.

_____
_____
_____

6. Glorifying God

The ultimate goal of our maturity and growth in love, excellence, integrity, and a fruitful life is God's glory and praise. We want to give the right opinion of God to every friend and family member God has brought into our lives. To glorify God is to give the right opinion of God. Our actions and attitudes should tell others that our Lord is a loving, excellent, holy, and gracious God. He wants us to grow in the graces that make up His character. Does your victory over sin speak of God's power? Does your kindness and love to others exemplify God's grace? Does your personal purity help you to magnify God's holiness? Do your life choices help others to see God?

"Lord, I want to grow. I pray that Your Spirit would produce in me a mature love, an excellent spirit, a testimony of integrity, and a fruitful life. Help me to grow and mature in these."

Saturday & Sunday
Review
Philippians 1:1-11

What did Philippians 1:1-2 teach you about Paul's confidence in God and his example of thanking God through serving others?

_____
_____
_____
_____
_____
_____
_____
_____
_____
_____

What did Philippians 1:3-4 teach you about Paul's confidence in God and his example of thanking God through praying?

_____
_____
_____
_____
_____
_____
_____
_____
_____
_____

What did Philippians 1:5-6 teach you about Paul's confidence in God and his example of thanking God through believing?

_____
_____
_____
_____
_____
_____
_____
_____
_____

What did Philippians 1:7-8 teach you about Paul's confidence in God and his example of thanking God through loving?

_____
_____
_____
_____
_____
_____
_____
_____
_____

What did Philippians 1:9-11 teach you about Paul's confidence in God and his example of thanking God through growing?

_____
_____
_____
_____
_____
_____
_____
_____
_____

WEEK 2: A GOD-CONFIDENCE GIVES ME A TRUSTING HEART.
MONDAY: Philippians 1:12-14

TRUST GOD IN THE FACE OF DIFFICULTIES

But I would ye should understand, brethren, that the things which happened unto me have fallen out rather unto the furtherance of the gospel; so that my bonds in Christ are manifest in all the palace, and in all other places; and many of the brethren in the Lord, waxing confident by my bonds, are much more bold to speak the word without fear.

1. What is Paul referring to when he said, **the things which happened unto me**? What **things**? What **things** could attempt to steal Paul's joy and confidence in God? Two times in the next two verses Paul gives us the answer...**my bonds**. Think about the greatest difficulty you are facing in your life and compare it with being chained to a soldier in prison. What is worse, friends not liking you or being handcuffed in jail? What is worse, being laughed at because you are a Christian or wondering if you will ever be free again? Most of us (including Paul) cannot change our difficult circumstances, but we can change our attitudes about our difficulties by keeping a proper focus. Paul faced difficulties with a God-confidence that enabled him to trust God with a joyful heart. Do you trust God with everything (yes, everything) in your life?

_____

_____

2. **The furtherance of the gospel** was not only Paul's goal, but his comfort as well. The difficulties he faced as a preacher and a prisoner not only enabled the gospel to be preached in some very unique places but encouraged timid believers to share Christ with a holy boldness. The word **furtherance** has the meaning of progress or advancement. The gospel is no good to anyone if it is kept in a secret box under lock and key. Do you remember the second verse of the little kids' Sunday school song, "Hide it under a bushel, No! I'm gonna let it shine!"? Romans 10:13-14 says, **For whosoever shall call upon the name of the Lord shall be saved. How then shall they call on Him in whom they have not believed? And how shall they believe in Him of whom they have not heard? And how shall they hear without a preacher?** According to this verse, how could **the furtherance of the gospel** be hindered?

_____

_____

What do you personally do to further the gospel?

_____

_____

3. **But I would ye should understand.** In other words Paul was saying, "My brothers and sisters in Christ, I want you to know the facts—not only what God is doing but why He is doing it." Nothing causes more heartache and confusion than rumors and gossip. When you hear the phrase, "Well, in my opinion..." get ready for some "advice" not supported by study, not based on research, and often not founded on biblical principles. The 1960s hosted a detective show with a character named Sergeant Friday who was famous for asking for "just the facts" and nothing more. Paul wanted his readers to understand the facts. Paul did not want anyone to feel sorry for him. Paul was not looking for pity. Paul could see the hand of God in his prison sentence and

wanted his friends in Philippi to see the same. Paul refused to focus on himself, but focused on God and the gospel. Describe some difficulty you have faced in the past and explain how the hand of God not only helped you through it, but grew you through it.

_____

_____

_____

4. **My bonds in Christ are manifest in all the palace, and in all other places.** In Romans 1:10 Paul prayed that by some means (if it was the will of God) he wanted to preach in Rome. Obviously, he did not know his preaching would be done from a prison rather than a pulpit, but Paul accepted what was thrown his way without complaint. It is amazing to see how God uses difficulties to get through doors otherwise shut to outsiders. Accidents and physical problems put us in rehabs and hospitals next to needy souls. God used Paul's chains to get the gospel into the high political offices in Rome. Can you think of any individual that God brought into your life through an unusual or even difficult situation? How has God used you to direct their thoughts to God?

_____

_____

_____

5. **Many brethren in the Lord, waxing confident by my bonds, are much more bold to speak the word without fear.** Some people fear heights. Others fear spiders. Many fear speaking in public. But most fear sharing Jesus Christ with unbelievers. Are you afraid to witness to your friends? Paul's gracious acceptance of his imprisonment put boldness and confidence into the hearts of his young converts. "If Paul can do it, so can I" seemed to be a motivating battle cry. I love the phrase **waxing confident**. We "wax confident" when we encourage others. We "wax confident" when we calm a troubled soul and encourage them to do right. We live in a world that is saturated with temptation. Evil is present behind doors one, two, and three. Our electronic world has made it easy to sin and hard to do right. So, what can we do? What did Paul do? Give up? No. Give in? No. Paul encouraged, motivated, and persuaded many by simply doing right regardless of the consequences (even prison). Who have you persuaded to walk with God, hate sin, and do right?

_____

_____

6. **Without fear.** Read 2 Timothy 1:7-8. Are you ashamed to be identified with Jesus Christ? Does it embarrass you when others find out that you are a Christian? Fear is a deceiving crippler. We must realize that fear does not come from God. We cannot blame it on personality, background, shyness, or disposition. Think of three individuals that need Christ and then pray specifically for each one. As you pray, pray that God will give you the boldness to share the truth with them without fear.

"Lord, I want to encourage others. Help me to accept the difficulties You have allowed in my life to persuade and motivate others to boldly live for You without fear."

WEEK 2: A GOD-CONFIDENCE GIVES ME A TRUSTING HEART.
TUESDAY: PHILIPPIANS 1:15-18

TRUST GOD IN THE FACE OF DISSENSION

Some indeed preach Christ even of envy and strife; and some also of good will: the one preach Christ of contention, not sincerely, supposing to add affliction to my bonds: but the other of love, knowing that I am set for the defence of the gospel. What then? Notwithstanding, every way, whether in pretence, or in truth, Christ is preached; and I therein do rejoice, yea, and will rejoice.

1. Paul finished verse 18 with the words, **I do rejoice and will rejoice!** It takes more than a prison, some chains, or some critical believers to steal Paul's joy away from him. He still had confidence in God. Your confidence in God will do the same for you. In our passage today, we catch a glimpse of a different kind of problem. We would expect unbelievers to attack those who have given their lives for the spread of the gospel, but not fellow believers. Have you ever been disappointed in another Christian friend who totally disagrees with your stand for God? Do you have friends that jokingly make fun of you because of your personal standards? How have you allowed any of them to steal your joy or dampen your zeal for God?

_____

_____

2. Paul described two kinds of believers, preachers, or ministries in verses 15-18.

   Contentious believers are full of envy, strife, and contention. They are not sincere, pretend to care but don't, and maliciously attack other believers.

   Comforting believers are full of love, good will, and truth. They genuinely support those who are declaring and defending the purity of the gospel.

The difference between the contentious believer and the comforting believer is not in what he teaches or believes, but how he teaches and believes it. Some can have strong biblical positions but drive others away with their harsh dispositions. If your theological position causes you to violate any other portion of Scripture, then there is something wrong with your position. If your theological position causes you to be mean, ugly, and unchristlike towards others, then you had better check your position. With this principle in mind, is there anything in your life or ministry that causes you to be harsh, ugly, or unchristlike? If so, what can you do about it and who do you need to go to for clarification, counsel, and maybe forgiveness?

_____

_____

3. **Envy.** Could you possibly be motivated by **envy**? Envy is a type of jealousy that actually causes you grief when you see the happiness of someone else. You not only want what they have, you maliciously don't want them to have it. Because of Paul's popularity and success, contentious believers started attacking him. Today the contentious ones would say, "Anyone who has that kind of crowd and is loved by so many must be doing something wrong." Envy is evil. Envy usually starts with comparisons that lead to complaining and criticizing. Envy is never satisfied. God's Word says, love envieth not! Who have you envied? Why were you so envious? What started the envy? How did you gain victory over the envy? How did your envy hurt yourself or others?

_____

_____

_____

4. Strife and contention. What do you do when your personal friends attack you and wonder what you have done wrong to be so successful in life. You can almost hear their attacks on Paul: "Paul's in prison. God must be punishing him for some secret sin in his life. If Paul's faith is so strong, how come he has not been released from jail? I'm not in jail. I must be better than him. Someday Paul will see that he is not the only big fish in this pond." Solomon told us years ago that only by pride (selfishness, selfish ambition) comes contention. If the stand you take at either your church, school, or work is causing division, hurt feelings, and daily disagreements, you had better check either the purity of your motives or the direction of those who are making trouble for you. Is your life surrounded by **strife** or **contention**? How does James counsel us to deal with these issues in James 3:13-18?

_____

_____

_____

5. Love and good will. Even though Paul had some ministry friends who were against him, he also had many comforting friends who were an encouragement to him. Their ministries were about others. They were consumed with "the cause" rather than "their cause" which they obviously learned from Paul himself. The key to getting along with co-laborers and other ministries is focus. A selfish focus leads to impressing others and building my own kingdom. A selfless focus causes me to please God and do my part for His kingdom. Paul and his comforting friends preached because they loved God and others. Whom do you love so much that you are willing to give them the truth even if it means jail time (or at least mocking time or being-laughed-at time)?

_____

_____

6. What then? These two little words say so much. You can almost hear Paul shaking his head and saying, "But what does it matter? Who cares if I am liked or not? Don't you realize that the truth of the gospel is being preached all over Philippi? I can't do it when I'm stuck here in prison with a rotating congregation of Roman soldiers. Those who think they are hurting me are only fooling themselves. They are doing what I would be doing if I was there. Preaching the gospel! This puts a smile both on my face and in my heart. **I do rejoice.** It takes more than a couple selfish attitudes to steal my joy. **I will rejoice!** My life's goal is being accomplished by others whom I have impacted in the past. They may not do it my way, but it is getting done. **I do rejoice and will rejoice.**" What keeps you rejoicing in the Lord?

_____

_____

"Lord, keep me rejoicing no matter who is attacking me. Keep me rejoicing no matter how difficult the opposition becomes. I am confident in You, Lord. Please, keep me rejoicing."

WEEK 2: A GOD-CONFIDENCE GIVES ME A TRUSTING HEART.
WEDNESDAY: PHILIPPIANS 1:18B-21

TRUST GOD IN THE FACE OF DEATH

I therein do rejoice, yea, and will rejoice. For I know that this shall turn to my salvation through your prayer, and the supply of the Spirit of Jesus Christ, according to my earnest expectation and my hope, that in nothing I shall be ashamed, but that with all boldness, as always, so now also Christ shall be magnified in my body, whether it be by life, or by death. For to me to live is Christ, and to die is gain.

1. If your goal in life is comfort, then discomfort becomes your enemy. If your life's goal is to be accepted, then anyone who rejects you is an enemy. If your goal in life is to stay alive, then death is your enemy. If your life's goal is that **Christ be magnified**, then your enemies seem to disappear. Whether it is comfort or discomfort, acceptance or rejection, life or death, Christ can use them all to magnify Himself. Paul's confidence in God enabled him to say, **I therein do rejoice, yea, and will rejoice.** Paul was in prison and still said, **I do rejoice**. Paul was not sure if he was going to get out of this one alive and said, **I will rejoice**. Basically, Paul was saying that whether he lived or died, or was released from prison or not, his joy could not be quenched. His trust in God's sovereign control enabled him to face death with a smile. How about you? Does death scare you? How do you personally deal with the thought of death?

_____

_____

2. **For I know that this shall turn to my salvation** (deliverance)**.** When Paul used the word **salvation** in verse 19, he was not referring to being saved from his sins by Christ's death, burial, and resurrection. Here **salvation** simply means deliverance. Paul rejoiced because he knew he was going to be delivered—either freed from prison to continue his ministry of preaching and encouraging or released from not only prison, but from life on this earth. One way or another, Paul was going to be free through the joint efforts of the prayers of God's people and the Spirit of God fulfilling the will of God. Remember, Paul's life focus and goal was for Jesus Christ to be magnified. There is no question that Paul wanted to get out of prison but he did not seem to care how he got out. What is your "prison" or situation in life that you would love to be delivered from? Why do you want to be delivered? How would you deliver yourself if you had the power? Is there any way your life's message and ministry is enhanced by your prison? These are not easy questions to answer. Think through them and write your meditative thoughts in a way that they could be an encouragement to someone who may be trapped and shackled in a similar prison.

_____

_____

3. **According to my earnest expectation and my hope, that in nothing I shall be ashamed.** Paul once again refuses to think about himself. He knew that he might soon die, but he did not know how. Paul lived in a day when torture was not uncommon. He prayed that he would have the sufficient courage and the holy boldness to take whatever came his way without being humiliated into saying something that would dishonor Christ. Paul trusted God but feared himself. Do you ever feel like that? You know that God is all-powerful, loving, and kind, but you fear that you are weak, unloving, harsh, and impatient. Paul seemed to fear that he might be tortured or pressured into dishonoring His Lord and Savior, Jesus Christ. Do you fear the same?

What would it take to make you turn on Christ? What kind of peer pressure would cause you to buckle? You may not be able to answer those questions regarding the future, but what about the past? Have you dishonored or denied the Lord? Do you buckle easily under peer pressure? Do you have friends who would love to turn you away from Christ? In the short passage we are studying today, how did Paul deal with such fears and concerns in his own heart?

_____

_____

4. **Whether it be by life, or by death; for to me to live is Christ, and to die is gain.** What we see as the ultimate "negative" in life is the ultimate "positive" in Paul's eyes. Sickness, pain, rejection, and loneliness still pale in comparison with death. Unlike most of us who would rather live, Paul would rather die! But he trusted God to do what was best. It is almost as if Paul was saying, "God, if you do what I want You to do, You'll take me to heaven with You. I want to die. Not only would I be free from this imprisonment, these chains, and the misery of my life being threatened with beatings and abuse, but I would be in Your presence and totally separated from sin and temptation. Forever! Lord, please take me to heaven which is 'far better' than any joy that I have ever experienced on this earth. Lord, I want to go home!" Can you pray that? That kind of prayer comes only from a heart that is totally confident in God. Do you fear death? Is it just the unknown you fear or are you fearful of your eternal destiny? At what age do most actually start looking forward to death? When their lifetime mate has gone before them? When they are facing such difficulties in life they want a release? When they know their Lord so well they can't wait to see Him? Why do you want to go to heaven?

_____

_____

5. God's view of death is quite different than ours. According to Ezekiel 33:11, **Say unto them, As I live, saith the Lord GOD, I have no pleasure in the death of the wicked; but that the wicked turn from his way and live: turn ye, turn ye from your evil ways...**and Psalm 116:15, **Precious in the sight of the LORD is the death of His saints**, how does God's view of believers and unbelievers differ?

_____

Christ shall be magnified, glorified, elevated, revered, preferred, lifted up, increased, honored, and exalted. Is this your purpose in life? It was Paul's!

"Lord, use my meager, insignificant life to glorify and magnify the name of Christ!"

WEEK 2: A GOD-CONFIDENCE GIVES ME A TRUSTING HEART.
THURSDAY: PHILIPPIANS 1:21-26

TRUST GOD IN THE FACE OF DILEMMA

For to me to live is Christ, and to die is gain. But if I live in the flesh, this is the fruit of my labor: yet what I shall choose I wot not. For I am in a strait betwixt two, having a desire to depart, and to be with Christ; which is far better: nevertheless to abide in the flesh is more needful for you. And having this confidence, I know that I shall abide and continue with you all for your furtherance and joy of faith; that your rejoicing may be more abundant in Jesus Christ for me by my coming to you again.

1. Life is full of dilemmas—not just deciding between the good and the bad, but deciding between the good and the good. The only way we can face tough decisions with confidence is to have a God-confidence that cannot be shaken. Paul faced a dilemma. Slowly read through the following meditation of our text today (Philippians 1:21-26) and put yourself in Paul's place.

For to me to live is Christ, (but if I had my choice) **to die is gain.** Now, I don't want to be selfish in this but I am actually being pulled in two different directions. One, I have **a desire to depart** (to die) **and to be with Christ (which is far better** than anything this world has to offer) **nevertheless** to stay alive, **to abide in** this old **flesh is more needful for you.** So I'm not going to fret or fear; I'm going to simply trust God! I know that God is in control and will do what is best for both you and me; I have **this confidence. I know that I shall abide and continue with you all for your furtherance and joy of faith; that your rejoicing may be more abundant in Jesus Christ for me by my coming to you again.** For you to experience the joy that I have in my heart, the joy that only God can give, I am confident in God that He wants me to be with you again before I go on to be with Him. That's fine with me. I'm going to rejoice either way, but this way we can rejoice together.

From our passage today, what dilemma was Paul wrestling with?

_____
_____
_____

2. Dilemmas. Decisions. Choices. Options.

> **I AM IN A STRAIT BETWIXT TWO. · I'M TORN BETWEEN TWO.**
> **WHAT I SHALL CHOOSE I WOT NOT. · I DON'T KNOW WHAT I WANT.**
> **I COULD EASILY GO EITHER WAY ON THIS ONE.**
> **I AM NOT SURE WHAT TO THINK. · THIS ONE STUMPS ME.**

Sometimes it is not easy to discern between what I want and what God wants. When faced with such dilemmas, we need to have some foundational principles to help us determine what is best. Paul gives us two supportive, foundational, practical principles to work from. By the way, these principles are repeated all throughout Scripture to keep us on the right path or to get us back on the right path. The first principle is from verses 22-23 and the second is from verses 24-26.

WHICH DECISION BEST USES MY GIFTS FOR CHRIST'S GLORY AND MAGNIFICATION (22-23)?

3. Paul wrote to the Corinthian believers and said, **Whether therefore ye eat, or drink, or whatsoever ye do, do all to the glory of God** (1 Corinthians 10:31). Earlier in the first chapter of Philippians Paul talked about **being filled with the fruits of righteousness, which are by Jesus Christ, unto the glory and praise of God** (Philippians 1:11). Jesus told His disciples in John 15:8, **Herein is my Father glorified, that ye bear much fruit; so shall ye be my disciples.** Paul was gifted by God to produce both the fruit of character and the fruit of converts that would bring glory to God. Many unbelievers were saved and trusting in God's grace because of Paul's incessant preaching and witness. Many believers were encouraged and challenged by Paul's fruit of character as they saw his love, joy, peace, patience, kindness, and faith. From Paul's testimony, they knew it was all because of God. God gifted Paul to do what he was called to do. How has God gifted you? In what way can your gifts and abilities bring praise and glory to the Lord? How are you going to use your God-given gifts in future service for the Lord?

_____
_____
_____

WHICH DECISION IS MOST NEEDFUL FOR THOSE GOD HAS CALLED ME TO SERVE (24-26)?

4. The word **nevertheless** is placed right between the explanation of Paul's desire and the explanation of the Philippians' needs. Sometimes as we focus on our desires God throws a **nevertheless** into our lives to remind us that our personal plans are not always His plans and may not always be best for us.

- Paul's desire was to depart to heaven (to die), **nevertheless**...
- Paul's desire was to be with Christ his Savior, **nevertheless**...
- Paul's desire was to experience a far better life in heaven, **nevertheless**...
- **Nevertheless,** to stay alive and keep serving is more needful for you.
- **Nevertheless,** to abide with you will help you grow in the Lord.
- **Nevertheless,** to continue with you for a while will increase your joyful faith.
- **Nevertheless,** to come to you again will increase your joy in Jesus Christ.

This will take some concentration, but think about a few personal desires that you have given up for family or friends as God put a **nevertheless** into your life. List them below and then take some time to think about how God's way is always superior to our way.

_____
_____
_____

"Lord, I don't always understand Your ways, but I trust You to use me in such a way that Your children will be encouraged and Your name will be glorified and magnified. Lord, use me."

WEEK 2: A GOD-CONFIDENCE GIVES ME A TRUSTING HEART.
FRIDAY: PHILIPPIANS 1:27-30

TRUST GOD IN THE FACE OF DISAGREEMENT

Only let your conversation be as it becometh the gospel of Christ: that whether I come and see you, or else be absent, I may hear of your affairs, that ye stand fast in one spirit, with one mind striving together for the faith of the gospel; and in nothing terrified by your adversaries: which is to them an evident token of perdition, but to you of salvation, and that of God. For unto you it is given in the behalf of Christ, not only to believe on Him, but also to suffer for His sake; having the same conflict which ye saw in me, and now hear to be in me.

1. Paul ends chapter one with biblical advice on how to deal with the adversary whose life's ambition is to be disagreeable. There will always be those who disagree with the way we live our lives, conduct our ministries, and worship our Lord. Instead of allowing them to control us, we can stay in control by using these principles.

- **MAKE THE GOSPEL LOOK GOOD TO YOUR DISAGREEABLE ADVERSARIES.**
- **REFUSE TO BE DIVIDED OR CONQUERED BY YOUR ADVERSARIES.**
- **LET YOUR CONFIDENCE AND ASSURANCE IN GOD IMPACT YOUR ADVERSARIES.**

Paul's disagreeables were unbelievers who were vehement in their ambition to keep Paul and the gospel quiet. Some of the same battle tactics used against Paul in Rome were being used in Philippi against the young Philippian believers. Who in your life antagonizes you for your strong witness as a Christian?

MAKE THE GOSPEL LOOK GOOD TO YOUR DISAGREEABLE ADVERSARIES.

2. **Let your conversation be as it becometh the gospel of Christ.** A compliment not often used today, "May I say you look quite becoming today!" conveys the fact that someone observed you, took notice of your appearance, and made an assessment. We want to live in such a way that we make the good news of salvation attractive to others. Let your life, your daily conduct, your consistent lifestyle (that others are watching) make the gospel of Christ appealing, delightful, and desirable. For instance, what we wear and what we say communicates what we want others to think about us. Would you be comfortable wearing nerdlike high-waters, bowling shirts, or polka-dot ties? Does it really express who and what you are? Regarding your appearance, what could you do to hide the fact that you are a conservative, committed Christian?

The word **conversation** can be translated either lifestyle or citizenship. It conveys the idea of living as a good citizen according to the customs and the laws of the state or to conduct your life according to the rules of the country where you live. There are definite differences in culture, customs, dress, and political views in different parts of the world. There is no way that those living in New York City, the Amazon jungle, and the Sahara desert would approach life the same. There are people in our world who believe in false gods, people who believe in no god, and others who believe in the one true God. Your lifestyle (**conversation**) displays to those around you where you are from and what you believe. How does your lifestyle coincide with your heavenly home and your committment to Jesus Christ as your personal Savior?

___

REFUSE TO BE DIVIDED OR CONQUERED BY YOUR ADVERSARIES.

3. There is strength in numbers and Christians need to stick together. The more we allow ourselves to be divided, the more susceptible we are to defeat. Paul urged the Philippians to be careful not to be **terrified**, frightened, or overly concerned by those who hate them. Being surrounded by friends helps to protect you from the opposition of your adversaries. Christians have a common goal...**the faith of the gospel**. With this goal in mind, verse 27 commands the Philippians to encourage each other with the same **mind** and **spirit**, **to stand** firm as one man and to be unmovable and unshakable. How can a group of good, loving friends help when someone mocks you or makes fun of you because of your outspoken faith in Jesus Christ?

___

LET YOUR CONFIDENCE AND ASSURANCE IN GOD IMPACT YOUR ADVERSARIES.

4. Read again Philippians 1:28-30. This is one of those passages that you have to read four or five times to completely understand it. You could paraphrase it this way.

> (Paul says) **which**, when they see your commitment to stand together for what you believe no matter how terrible the persecution becomes, it **is** a sign **to them** (even proof) of their own destruction; while at the same time it gives you the assurance **of** your **salvation**, the proof that you are saved, and that your salvation comes from **God** and God alone. **For** as a Christian, **it** has been granted or **given** to **you**, on **behalf of Christ**, **not only to believe on Him, but also to suffer for His sake**, experiencing the very **same conflict that you saw me** experience **and now hear** that I am experiencing again.

This **conflict** could be referring to the persecution Paul experienced on his first visit to Philippi as explained in Acts 16. After being dragged through the market, Paul and Silas were falsely accused by the masters of the demon-possessed girl that Paul restored. The magistrates tore their robes off them, repeatedly struck them, and threw them into prison with their feet fastened in stocks. When Paul said, **and now hear to be in me,** he was probably referring to his present sufferings in the Roman prison. Paul's response was to sing and his reaction was to praise God, both of which impacted his adversaries for Christ. How do you respond when you are mocked or misunderstood because of your stand for Christ?

___

"Lord, as I strive to stand for You, I know there will be many who will disagree and attempt to hinder Your work. Help me to make the gospel look good in their eyes by my godly response."

Saturday & Sunday
Review

Philippians 1:12-30

What did Philippians 1:12-14 teach you about Paul's confidence in God as he trusted God in the face of great difficulties?

_____

What did Philippians 1:15-18 teach you about Paul's confidence in God as he trusted God in the face of divisive dissension?

_____

What did Philippians 1:18b-21 teach you about Paul's confidence in God as he trusted God in the face of death?

What did Philippians 1:21-26 teach you about Paul's confidence in God as he trusted God in the face of a difficult dilemma?

What did Philippians 1:27-30 teach you about Paul's confidence in God as he trusted God in the face of disagreement?

Principle Two:

An Unselfish Spirit Produces Unspeakable Joy!

Philippians 2:1-30

Week 3: The Attitude of an Unselfish Christ.
Monday: Philippians 2:1-2

The Heart of an Unselfish Christ

If there be therefore any consolation in Christ, if any comfort of love, if any fellowship of the Spirit, if any bowels and mercies, fulfil ye my joy, that ye be likeminded, having the same love, being of one accord, of one mind.

If you have ever been consoled or encouraged **in Christ**, if you have been **comforted** by His **love**, **if** you have enjoyed **fellowship** with **the Spirit** of Christ who lives within you by spending time together through prayer and the Word, **if** you have sensed His tender affection, patient compassion, and loving **mercies** toward you, then you will make **my joy** complete (which will also fill your heart with joy) by being **likeminded** with Christ (for you to be a blessing to others like Christ has been to you). Have **the same love** (comfort and encourage others with the same love that Christ loved you); **be of one accord** (purpose to be agreeable by viewing each situation from everyone's vantage point) **and of one mind** (think together in a way that your opinions mesh with each other).

1. The key word in these two familiar verses is **likeminded**. It combines the two words *phroneo* (to think) with *autos* (self: this "self" is referring to Christ Himself) which results in **likeminded**, or thinking like Christ Himself. What a challenge! In just forty-three simple words Paul tells us what Christ has done for us and what we should do for others. You can't miss this one.

The What: An Unselfish Mandate

- Calmly encourage others like Christ calmly encourages you.
- Lovingly comfort others like Christ lovingly comforts you.
- Eagerly fellowship with others like Christ eagerly fellowships with you.
- Tenderly love others like Christ tenderly loves you.

The How: An Unselfish Methodology

- Love each other.
- Agree with each other.
- Think with each other.

List three individuals (family or friends) that you can practice these principles on.

The What: An Unselfish Mandate

Calmly encourage others like Christ calmly encourages you.

2. Christ, a master encourager, uses His Word (the Bible) to encourage us. **For whatsoever things were written aforetime were written for our learning, that we through patience and comfort of the Scriptures might have hope** (Romans 15:4). For those who fear death Christ gives Psalm 23. For those who struggle with forgiveness He directs them to Psalm 38, Psalm 51, and Psalm 32. Where in God's Word would you direct one of your three friends listed above who struggles with fear and worry?

LOVINGLY COMFORT OTHERS LIKE CHRIST LOVINGLY COMFORTS YOU.

3. The word used for **comfort** (*paramuthian*) in this phrase actually refers to comforting through spoken words. It is that comforting word at just the right time that encourages the hurting person to refocus on the goodness of the Lord. Describe the last time that someone needed comfort and God gave you the exact words at just the right time to calm their heart?

_____

_____

We cannot leave this principle without carefully meditating on 2 Corinthians 1:3-5.

Blessed be God, even the Father of our Lord Jesus Christ, the Father of mercies, and the God of all comfort; Who comforteth us in all our tribulation, that we may be able to comfort them which are in any trouble, by the comfort wherewith we ourselves are comforted of God. For as the sufferings of Christ abound in us, so our consolation also aboundeth by Christ.

EAGERLY FELLOWSHIP WITH OTHERS LIKE CHRIST EAGERLY FELLOWSHIPS WITH YOU.

4. Fellowship conveys the idea of sharing and communing which presupposes spending time together. We fellowship with Christ as we spend time with Him in prayer and Bible meditation. According to 1 John 1:3, 6-7, what could hinder our fellowship with God and others?

_____

...truly our fellowship is with the Father, and with His Son Jesus Christ...If we say that we have fellowship with Him, and walk in darkness, we lie, and do not the truth: but if we walk in the light, as He is in the light, we have fellowship one with another, and the blood of Jesus Christ His Son cleanseth us from all sin.

TENDERLY LOVE OTHERS LIKE CHRIST TENDERLY LOVES YOU.

5. The phrase **bowels and mercies** is not commonly found in many e-mails or text messages today. This phrase refers to the innermost, deep-down feelings or affections. Today we would say, "I love you from the bottom of my heart." This kind of love cannot be faked or manufactured. It is a love that overflows from Christ's love for us. People know when you care. Are you a loving person? Can you love someone even when they disagree with you? In a practical way, how can you do this?

_____

_____

THE HOW: AN UNSELFISH METHODOLOGY

LOVE EACH OTHER. AGREE WITH EACH OTHER. THINK WITH EACH OTHER.

6. Paul was so like-minded with Christ that his heart was completely filled with joy when those he encouraged, comforted, fellowshipped with, and loved were willing to follow his example as he followed Christ's. This is major spiritual growth!

- Have the **same love** (comfort others with the same love that Christ loved you).

- Be of **one accord** (purpose to be agreeable by considering each viewpoint).

- Be of **one mind** (think together in a way that your opinions mesh with each other).

Without compromising your principles, how can you use this unselfish methodology with the three individuals you listed in our study today?

_____

_____

"Lord, You encourage, comfort, and love me. Help me do the same for others."

Week 3: The attitude of an unselfish Christ.
Tuesday: Philippians 2:3-4

The motivation of an unselfish Christ

Let nothing be done through strife or vainglory; but in lowliness of mind let each esteem other better than themselves. Look not every man on his own things, but every man also on the things of others.

To be **likeminded** with Christ and to live with the same unselfish attitude that Christ had; do **nothing** (nothing at all) that is motivated by self-centered **strife**, selfish ambition, or self-seeking rivalry. Do **nothing** that is motivated by empty, **vain**, prideful, desire for praise or self **glory**. Instead, with a true heartfelt humility **of mind** (the **lowliness of mind** that Christ exemplified) consider **others** as more important, and actually **better than** yourselves. Do **not** be consumed with your **own** self interests and your **own things**, **but** train your mind to be interested in the needs and interests **of others**. Put their interests before your own.

1. Have you ever struggled with a selfish attitude? It is much easier to keep your focus on yourself than on others. Most of us want what we want, when we want it, and how we want it regardless of how it affects anyone else. If someone in your family or one of your closest friends were asked if you were selfish, what would they say? You do not have to look too far to find someone more selfish than yourself (although that person may be thinking the same about you). What is the first thing that caught your attention as you read the meditation of Philippians 2:3-4 above?

_____

_____

2. Has anyone ever accused you of having an attitude? An attitude could be considered your response (often nonverbal) to a given situation based on your personal view or opinion. Attitudes can be both good and bad. Your attitude (the way you think) controls your actions (the way you behave). The motivation of an unselfish attitude starts with the phrase, **Let nothing be done through strife or vainglory**. The word translated **strife** means much more than simply quarreling or arguing. It actually implies "selfish ambition" and can convey the ideas of either canvassing for political office (as a politician) or selling for personal gain (as a salesman). When you are a salesman, everyone becomes a customer. Politicians see people as votes. Unselfish, Christlike servants see others as needy souls. How do you look at others? Are they here to make you successful and feel good about yourself or are you here to make them successful and fulfilled? Your attitude toward others will impact your actions toward them. So, in what ways are you motivated by selfish ambition (**strife**)?

_____

_____

3. The next word that helps us clarify a selfish attitude is **vainglory**. This word has the idea of being self-conceited, empty, or undeservingly desirous of praise or attention. Without listing any names, do you know anyone who is motivated by **vainglory**? What gives you that impression? What do you see in their lives that would make you think they expect praise and attention but are blinded to their true gifts or abilities? As you answer these questions, could anyone say this about you?

_____

_____

4. Learning to live with an unselfish attitude continues with the phrase, **but in lowliness of mind let each esteem other better than themselves.** You cannot esteem others when you esteem yourself. To **esteem** is to bring to the forefront of the mind. It is all you think about. **Lowliness of mind** fights against pride and haughtiness focusing on others. When your parents hung out with you at Toys"R"Us or sat through your second grade piano recital, they were definitely esteeming you (and what you liked to do) above themselves (and what they liked to do). If you are a child or a teen living at home, how can you do the same for your parents?

_____

_____

5. Finally, learning to live with an unselfish attitude implores us to, **Look not every man on his own things, but every man also on the things of others.** Taken out of context, this could be a confusing verse. Standing alone it could mean, "Be discontent with what you have and look at what others have" or "The grass is always greener on the other side of the fence." What Paul is actually saying here flows with what we have already seen regarding unselfish motivation.

1. **DON'T SEEK TO PLEASE YOURSELF (PHILIPPIANS 2:3A).**
2. **VIEW OTHERS AS BETTER THAN YOURSELF (PHILIPPIANS 2:3B).**
3. **LOOK OUT FOR THE INTERESTS OF OTHERS (AND NOT YOUR OWN) (PHILIPPIANS 2:4).**

This is not easy! This is not easy for anyone! Compare your selfishness with the unselfishness of Christ and you will be overwhelmed with how selfish you really are. Christ exemplified an unselfish attitude in every choice that He made including coming to earth and dying for you and me. That's unselfish. In what way did Christ model such unselfishness in the following two verses (and can we model the same)?

Even as the Son of man came not to be ministered unto, but to minister, and to give His life a ransom for many (Matthew 20:28).

_____

_____

For Christ also hath once suffered for sins, the just for the unjust, that He might bring us to God, being put to death in the flesh, but quickened by the Spirit (1 Peter 3:18).

_____

_____

"Lord, I am selfish and I know it. Please help me to seek to please others, view others better than myself, and look out for their interests and not my own. Please help my selfish heart!"

WEEK 3: THE ATTITUDE OF AN UNSELFISH CHRIST.
WEDNESDAY: PHILIPPIANS 2:5-6

THE MIND OF AN UNSELFISH CHRIST

Let this mind be in you, which was also in Christ Jesus: Who, being in the form of God, thought it not robbery to be equal with God.

Keep the same unselfish attitude and humble mind-set in yourself that **Christ Jesus** had while He lived here on earth. He was God, yet He humbled Himself! What do you have to glory in or be proud about that you have not received from God? **Who, being in the form** and the very nature **of God** did not consider or think His equality **with God** was something to be grasped or held on to but willingly let it go for the good of those He came to save.

1. **Let this mind be in you.** What kind of **mind** do you have? Some keep their minds under control while others constantly wrestle with selfish and sensual thinking. All temptation starts in the mind. Your thoughts are an index to your character. The battle of the mind is one of the greatest battles you will ever face. Why? Because you are what you think! Solomon reminds us, **as a man thinketh in his heart so is he**. What you are thinking today you are becoming tomorrow. With all these thoughts in mind, how does your mind resemble or contradict the mind of Christ Jesus?

_____

_____

2. **Let this mind be in you, which was also in Christ Jesus.** We can never really know what someone is thinking unless they tell us. All of us have habits, fears, biblical truths, and unbiblical desires that keep our minds thinking the way they do. We know that the **mind of Christ** (the way Christ thought) is described, defined, and illustrated throughout His Word. For instance, study Jonah to see how God thought about a rebellious prophet. Read the "Sermon on the Mount" to learn how Christ handled ordinary issues of life. Christ's Word is Christ's mind. Briefly explain what you do each day to allow the Word of God to change your mind to think like the mind of Christ.

_____

_____

3. **Who,** (while in the flesh as a man on earth) **being in the form of God, thought it not robbery to be equal with God.** At Christmastime, with the focus on Christ's coming to earth as a baby in a Bethlehem manger surrounded by angels, shepherds, and animals, it is easy to casually glance over the incredible impact of the incarnation of Jesus Christ (when Jesus took on human flesh and became a man). God, in the bodily presence of Jesus Christ, came to do what no mere man could do—live a perfect life and pay sin's penalty. Commentator John MacArthur states it so well:

"The incarnation is the central miracle of Christianity, the most grand and wonderful of all the things that God has ever done. That miracle of miracles is the theme of Philippians 2:5-8. Some scholars believe this passage was originally a hymn, sung by early Christians to commemorate and celebrate the incarnation of the Son of God. It has been called a Christological gem, a theological diamond that perhaps sparkles brighter than any other in Scripture. In a simple, brief, yet extraordinarily profound way, it describes the condescension of the second Person of the Trinity to be born, to live, and to die in human form to provide redemption for fallen mankind. The Incarnation calls believers to follow Jesus' incomparable example of humble self-denial, self-giving, self-sacrifice, and selfless love as He lived out the Incarnation in obedient submission to His Father's will."

(*Philippians*, Moody Press, John MacArthur, Jr)

Would you be willing to live three years as a slave to a wealthy landowner in Central Africa? Would you be willing to put everything you have (clothes, computers, cars, cell phones) in a storage container and live alongside the street people of New York City? Would you be willing to say "good-bye" to all the comforts of home and live with an Amazonian tribe for the next three years? What are some of the things that Jesus Christ left in heaven when He came to earth over 2000 years ago?

_____

_____

What are some of the difficulties and misunderstandings He might have faced as a poor carpenter's son that He would have never experienced in heaven?

_____

Describe some of the physical trauma Jesus Christ suffered the week before His death on the cross that He would have never suffered if He had chosen not to come to earth as a man to save you and me from our sins?

_____

_____

4. [Jesus Christ], **being in the form of God, thought it not robbery to be equal with God.** Jesus Christ is God. He was not stealing any of God's glory by saying He was God and was equal with God. Just as Christ was **in the form of God** (verse 6), He took upon Himself **the form of a servant** (verse 7). He was both God and Man. We should never emphasize His humanity with disregard to His divinity. Being in the form of God, He chose to be humbled into the form of a man. It was thirty-three years later when He left His vile, weak, fleshly body for His glorified body. How does all of this apply to us today? What practical application can we learn from Christ's incarnation? Christ left all to become nothing. We are nothing (but think we are something) and are not even willing to lay aside our nothingness for others! Ask yourself the following questions to see just how much you are willing to be like-minded with Christ.

• What is so important to me that I am not willing to give up for the salvation and success of others?

_____

_____

• In what way do I view myself better than someone else and would cringe at the thought of becoming like them in order to serve them?

_____

_____

• Do I live with the unselfish mind of Christ?

_____

_____

"Lord, I struggle with selfish thinking. You unselfishly left all for me. Help me to get my mind off myself and think of You and others. Help me to think like You."

WEEK 3: THE ATTITUDE OF AN UNSELFISH CHRIST.
THURSDAY: PHILIPPIANS 2:7-8

THE HUMILITY OF AN UNSELFISH CHRIST

But made Himself of no reputation, and took upon Him the form of a servant, and was made in the likeness of men: and being found in fashion as a man, He humbled Himself, and became obedient unto death, even the death of the cross.

[Even though Christ was equal with God] He made **Himself** as nothing; He voluntarily emptied Himself of anything that would cause recognition as God or give Him the **reputation** that He was God, **and took upon** Himself **the** bodily **form of a** bondservant (a man who chooses to be a slave out of love or loyalty) **and was made in the likeness** or form **of men, and being found in** appearance or fashioned like **a man,** He willingly **humbled Himself** by becoming **obedient** to the wishes of evil men who wanted to kill Him by one of the most horrific means of **death** any man could ever experience—death by crucifixion **on a cross**.

1. We will never fully comprehend what took place when Christ left the glories of heaven and became a man. He still was God and never stopped being God, but did become a man. Spiros Zodhiates' word study helps us get a better grasp of what happened 2000 years ago.

> "[Christ's] humanity did not displace deity in His personality. Rather He took upon Himself voluntarily, in addition to His preincarnate condition, something which veiled His deity. Proper recognition is called dóxa, glory, praise, from the verb dokéœ, to recognize. In the form of man and servant, He lacked the recognition among men that He had with the Father (John 17:5). This voluntary humiliation of Christ began with the incarnation and was carried through to His crucifixion. In His resurrection, He laid aside His form of a servant."
> (*The Complete Word Study Dictionary*, Spiros Zodhiates, 1992, AMG International)

But made Himself of no reputation. If we are to ever experience the outrageous, contagious joy that Paul refers to throughout Philippians, we must be willing to live with the same kind of unselfish attitude that Christ lived with. Jesus Christ willingly and voluntarily emptied Himself of anything that would give Him acceptance and popularity. Most of us want to be accepted. Most of us want to be liked by many (be popular). Most of us hate the thought of being rejected or pushed out of the group. For years, Jesus did everything He could to keep His divinity masked by His humanity. Many today do everything they can to make others think they are something that they are really not! How do dress standards or music standards affect our desire to be accepted? How could drinking and illegal drugs impact a desire to have a cool reputation? In what way could immorality be a part of the desire to be known, popular, and liked? What are many willing to do just to be liked and accepted?

_____

_____

_____

2. **And took upon Him the form of a servant.** Jesus was willing to become a slave, lower than ordinary man. The slaves of Bible times were often treated as nothing more than animals to be used, abused, and thrown away. Most slaves would never have chosen that life for themselves,

but Jesus did. Most men are not willing to be looked down on, despised, and treated with absolutely no respect, but Jesus was. Why? Why a slave? To have the greatest impact on others Jesus humbled Himself to the greatest degree. Finish some of the statements below that Jesus made on how serving others is superior to being served by others. (By the way, Paul learned this well as seen in 1 Corinthians 9:19, 2 Corinthians 2:5, and Galatians 5:13.)

• Matthew 20:27 **And whosoever will be chief among you**

_____

_____

• Matthew 20:28 **Even as the Son of man came not to be ministered unto** (served)

_____

• Matthew 23:11 **But he that is greatest among you**

_____

_____

• Matthew 23:12 **And whosoever shall exalt himself shall be abased**

_____

_____

• John 13:14-15 **If I then, your Lord and Master, have washed your feet**

_____

_____

3. **He humbled Himself, and became obedient unto death, even the death of the cross.** God treated Christ as a sinner so He could treat sinners like Christ. The joy-producing attitude of humility that Christ exemplified reaches its peak at His voluntary death on the cross. He could have been beheaded like John the Baptist, stoned like Stephen, left for dead on a remote island like John, but was willingly crucified. Death by crucifixion was probably the most painful and shameful form of execution ever devised by man. It was a form of torture normally reserved for the vilest of criminals and the lowest of all mankind. Jesus chose the most horrific form of death imaginable to show God's detestation for sin. Jesus submitted to the most embarrassing and humiliating public forms of execution to expose the ultimate shame that sin produces in a life. Hebrews 12:2 tells us that...**for the joy that was set before Him endured the cross, despising the shame, and is set down at the right hand of the throne of God.** The word **despising** does not mean hating, but viewing as nothing. Jesus looked at all the torture, pain, humiliation, and shame as nothing in light of paying the price of sin for you and me. Meditate on Christ's death and write a prayer of thanksgiving and praise to Jesus for humbling Himself for you. (To help your meditation, refer to John 19, Matthew 27, and Mark 15.)

_____

_____

_____

_____

"Lord, You willingly humbled Yourself, suffered, and died for me. You didn't care what others said or thought. Please, Lord, help me to learn from Your humble, unselfish attitude."

WEEK 3: THE ATTITUDE OF AN UNSELFISH CHRIST.
FRIDAY: PHILIPPIANS 2:9-11

THE GLORY OF AN UNSELFISH CHRIST

Wherefore God also hath highly exalted Him, and given Him a name which is above every name: that at the name of Jesus every knee should bow, of things in heaven, and things in earth, and things under the earth; and that every tongue should confess that Jesus Christ is Lord, to the glory of God the Father.

[Jesus Christ, as **God, made Himself** nothing, willingly **humbled Himself** to **the death of the cross] wherefore**, for this reason, **God highly exalted Him** and gave **Him a name** that **is above every** other **name** in existence, so **that at the name of Jesus every knee** of every believer and every nonbeliever who are **in heaven**, on **earth**, **and under the earth** will **bow, and every tongue** of every believer and every nonbeliever will **confess,** admit, and say with confidence **that Jesus Christ is Lord, to the glory,** honor, and praise **of God the Father.**

1. We live in a day of self-love, self-worth, and self-exaltation (selfishness). How do most of your friends or acquaintances show that they are consumed with their own self-worth and self-exaltation?

_____

_____

We often forget the simple principle Jesus gave us in Dr. Luke's gospel as He described the prayer of penitent sinner. **And the publican, standing afar off, would not lift up so much as his eyes unto heaven, but smote upon his breast, saying, God be merciful to me a sinner. I tell you, this man went down to his house justified rather than the other: for every one that exalteth himself shall be abased; and he that humbleth himself shall be exalted** (Luke 18:13-14). Not only does Philippians 2:9-11 teach the exaltation of Jesus Christ, it also teaches the principle that those of us who are willing to humble ourselves before God will be exalted in some way at some time. Finish the verses where both James and Peter shared this same principle of humility with those they encouraged.

• James 4:6 **But He giveth more grace. Wherefore He saith,**

_____

_____

• James 4:10 **Humble yourselves in the sight of the Lord,**

_____

_____

• 1 Peter 5:5-6 **Likewise, ye younger, submit yourselves unto the elder. Yea, all of you be subject one to another, and be clothed with humility:**

_____

_____

Humble yourselves therefore under the mighty hand of God,

_____

_____

2. **And given Him a name which is above every name, that at the name of Jesus every knee should bow.** No one was more humiliated and despised than Jesus Christ. No one has been or ever will be exalted like Jesus Christ. Every proud, arrogant, agnostic, or atheistic unbeliever who personally exalted himself above our Lord by mocking, ridiculing, and rejecting Jesus Christ will be slammed down to reality as they bow before Jesus in humility. One day the Herods, the Hitlers, the Stalins, and the Husseins of our history who exalted themselves above God, denying the truth of God's Word, will bow in utter submission to Jesus Christ as Lord. That day will come and may be closer than any of us realize. We do not need to wait for that day to humbly bow before the Lord. Our unselfish humility (that which we have learned from Christ Himself) should cause us to humbly bow every day. List three or four of the practical ways from 1 Peter 5:5-11 we can humble ourselves before God.

Likewise, ye younger, submit yourselves unto the elder. Yea, all of you be subject one to another, and be clothed with humility: for God resisteth the proud, and giveth grace to the humble. Humble yourselves therefore under the mighty hand of God, that He may exalt you in due time: casting all your care upon Him; for He careth for you. Be sober, be vigilant; because your adversary the devil, as a roaring lion, walketh about, seeking whom he may devour: whom resist stedfast in the faith, knowing that the same afflictions are accomplished in your brethren that are in the world. But the God of all grace, who hath called us unto His eternal glory by Christ Jesus, after that ye have suffered a while, make you perfect, stablish, strengthen, settle you. To Him be glory and dominion for ever and ever. Amen.

_____
_____

3. **And that every tongue should confess that Jesus Christ is Lord, to the glory of God the Father.** Jesus Christ is LORD! Lord conveys the idea of majesty, authority, and sovereignty. Someday, Jesus will be called the **Lord of lords and King of kings** as we read in Revelation 19:16. We do not have to wait until the battle of Armageddon when all the anti-God nations of the world are overthrown by Jesus Christ Himself to honor Him as Lord. If Jesus Christ is your Lord then He is your Master. Do you allow Jesus Christ to have ultimate authority in your life? Do you honor Him as a majestic King? Do you believe that this sovereign Lord has total control of your life? What are some of the areas of your life that you struggle in giving Jesus Christ total control of? What area of your personal life do you refuse to give up or give over to God? In what way do you insist on being in control (master) of your own life?

_____
_____
_____
_____

"Lord, Your voluntary humiliation and condescension for me should motivate my heart to willingly and humbly submit to You as Lord, Master, and King. Help me to humble myself."

Saturday & Sunday
Review

Philippians 2:1-11

What did Philippians 2:1-2 teach you about having an unselfish spirit as you carefully studied the heart of an unselfish Christ?

What did Philippians 2:3-4 teach you about having an unselfish spirit as you carefully studied the motivation of an unselfish Christ?

What did Philippians 2:5-6 teach you about having an unselfish spirit as you carefully studied the mind of an unselfish Christ?

What did Philippians 2:7-8 teach you about having an unselfish spirit as you carefully studied the humility of an unselfish Christ?

What did Philippians 2:9-11 teach you about having an unselfish spirit as you carefully studied the glory of an unselfish Christ?

WEEK 4: THE ATTITUDE OF AN UNSELFISH CHRISTIAN.
MONDAY: PHILIPPIANS 2:12-13

THE UNSELFISH ATTITUDE OF AN OBEDIENT BELIEVER

Wherefore, my beloved, as ye have always obeyed, not as in my presence only, but now much more in my absence, work out your own salvation with fear and trembling. For it is God which worketh in you both to will and to do of His good pleasure.

[Because **Jesus Christ** has been **exalted and every knee** will **bow** to Him] for this reason, **my** dearly **beloved** friends, **as** you **have always obeyed** (**not only in my presence** when I was right there watching over you, **but now much more in my absence** when I will not know whether you obey or not), **work out of your own salvation** by practicing an obedience that is based on a **fear and trembling** of the weakness of your flesh and the power of temptation; (but don't despair or give up) **for it is God who works in you both to will** (He will give you the desire) **and to do** (He will give you the power) to fulfill or to do **His good pleasure** or that which pleases Him.

1. **Wherefore, my beloved, as ye have always obeyed.** The phrase "Obedience is the very best way to show that you believe" is not just the first line of Patch the Pirate's children's song entitled "Obedience," but a foundational principle for life. Paul teaches both the Philippians and us three simple truths on obedience in these verses.

OBEY WHEN NO ONE IS WATCHING.

OBEY WITH THE RIGHT HEART MOTIVATION.

OBEY WITH THE STRENGTH THAT GOD GIVES YOU.

Which one of these three principles do you struggle with the most and why?

_____

OBEY WHEN NO ONE IS WATCHING.

2. **Not as in my presence only, but now much more in my absence.** Do you (or did you if you are no longer a teen) obey differently when your parents are around than when they are gone to work? Do your actions change when a teacher or an employer leaves the room? Have you ever done anything in secret that you would not have done if you knew someone was watching? Do you remember the sudden fear in your stomach when a parent or an authority caught you stealing, cheating, lying, or watching something that you shouldn't? Paul actually praised the Philippians for obeying when he was not there to check up on them. Could he say the same about you? We often forget Solomon's advice in Proverbs 15:3, **The eyes of the LORD are in every place, beholding the evil and the good.** Look up the following passages and explain how they should impact our obedience when there is no one around to watch or see us.

• 2 Chronicles 16:9

_____
_____

• Job 34:21-22

_____
_____

• Proverbs 5:21

_____

_____

OBEY WITH THE RIGHT HEART MOTIVATION.

3. **Work out your own salvation with fear and trembling.** This nine-word phrase has been misunderstood by many over the years. It has nothing to do with "works-salvation" where you need to do something to earn God's favor. You can't! God's salvation is truly a gift that cannot be earned or worked for. Thayer's word study says **fear and trembling** are used to describe the anxiety of one who distrusts his ability completely to meet all requirements, but religiously does his utmost to fulfill his duty. MacArthur's commentary says that **fear and trembling** are proper reactions to one's own spiritual weakness and the power of temptation. Actually, it is a variation of the little train that said, "I think I can. I think I can." Instead we are to say, "I know I can't. I know God can. I know I can't. I know God can." We are weak. Temptation is strong. Aside from God's enablement we could never say "no" to temptation. How could this simple truth apply to your greatest spiritual struggle or temptation?

_____

_____

_____

When Paul used the words **work out**, he was implying that living for God is hard work. No one said it was easy! MacArthur's commentary explains it this way.

"Everything in life requires energy. It takes energy to walk and to work. It takes energy to think and to meditate. It takes energy to obey and to worship God. It takes spiritual energy to grow as a Christian, to live a life that is holy, fruitful, and pleasing to the Lord. The main verb 'work out' calls for the constant energy and effort necessary to finish a task."
(*Philippians*, Moody Press, John MacArthur)

OBEY WITH THE STRENGTH THAT GOD GIVES YOU.

4. **For it is God which worketh in you both to will and to do of His good pleasure.** Philippians 2:13 is one of the most comforting verses in Scripture. God will give us the desire (the want to) and the power (the how to) to do His will. Since it is not you doing the work in your own strength, then if you are not working, laboring, and toiling for your Lord, you obviously are fighting the Spirit of God who is in you. God's grace is evident when your heart is filled with a desire to please Him. God's grace is at work in your life when you look temptation or trials directly in the face and handle them in a way that pleases God. Describe the last time you personally experienced such grace in your life.

_____

_____

_____

Obedience is the very best way to show that you believe. Obey God! How?

Obey when no one is watching.

Obey with the right heart motivation.

Obey with the strength that God gives you.

"Lord, thank You for the power and the desire to do Your will. Thank you for enabling me to obey in a way that brings good pleasure to You."

Week 4: The attitude of an unselfish Christian.
Tuesday: Philippians 2:14-15

The unselfish attitude of a blameless child

> *Do all things without murmurings and disputings: that ye may be blameless and harmless, the sons of God, without rebuke, in the midst of a crooked and perverse nation, among whom ye shine as lights in the world.*

Everything you face in life should be done **without** grumbling, griping, complaining, **murmuring**, arguing, **disputing**, debating, and questioning. Prove that you are the true children **of God** who are **blameless, harmless**, pure, innocent, **without rebuke**, above reproach, **in the midst** (right in the middle where you can be seen, gawked at, scrutinized, and examined from every side) **of a crooked** (warped toward wickedness; bent toward evil) **and perverse** (turned or twisted away from truth) **generation, among whom** you stand out **as** bright, shining **lights in the world**.

1. **Do all things without murmurings and disputings.** Selfish teens and self-centered adults complain about everything. Nothing is ever good enough for them. The words "murmur" and "whine" are tagged by our English grammarians as onomatopoeias, or, words that sound like they read. The word "murmur" repeats the same syllable in a grumbling sort of way. The word "whining" is hard to say without a high-pitched nasal sound to it. Are you a whiner and a murmurer? Do you gripe about not having anything to wear? Do you complain about too much homework? Do you debate and question your authorities? Why? Why would any unselfish believer gripe, complain, whine, murmur, argue, or grumble? Truthfully, "unselfish believers" would not, but selfish individuals live in that I-will-never-be-happy-satisfied-or-content world. How could the following six attitudes change a once contented, grateful heart to a murmuring, complaining heart?

• Discontent

_____

• Holding a grudge

_____

• Bitterness

_____

• Haughty, arrogant spirit

_____

• Ingratitude

_____

• Selfishness

_____

2. Why? Why is it so important to refuse to murmur or complain? Paul answers the question in the next phrase, **that ye may be blameless and harmless, the sons of God, without rebuke** living in the middle of a crooked, perverse world that is consumed with griping and complaining. In

other words, to prove that you are different! Unselfish children of God should be nothing (yes, nothing) like this selfish world we live in. Prove to everyone you know at work or at school that you are a **blameless, harmless**, pure, innocent Christian. If you live this way, you will be (as Paul puts it) **without rebuke** (above reproach) and no one will be able to point a finger at you and say, "See, you're no different than anyone else. What good is your Christianity? I'm every bit as good as you! In fact, if your God is so good, why do you gripe and complain about everything?" Describe how this same scenario has happened to one of your friends (or even yourself) and hurt their testimony as a Christian.

_____
_____
_____

3. The spotlight is on you, Christian! This unselfish, uncomplaining, unmurmuring (is that a word?) lifestyle is to be lived **in the midst of a crooked and perverse nation, among whom ye shine as lights in the world. In the midst** (right in the middle where you can be seen, gawked at, scrutinized, and examined from every side) **of a crooked** (warped toward wickedness; bent toward evil) **and perverse** (turned or twisted away from truth) **generation.** You have to study YOUR generation (your multitude of contemporaries) to understand how to keep straight what is being twisted and turned. Your parents' generation (if you are a teen) rebelled against the rules. Your generation simply states there are no rules—no rules for morality, no rules for marriage, no rules for right. **Among whom** you appear **as lights in the world**. It is in this crooked, truth-twisting, dark generation that blameless, pure, innocent Christians must appear as bright lights. The shocking reality of the unperverted, untwisted, absolute truth of God's Word is the only light left in this increasingly dark world. You can't be a blameless bright light and complain at the same time. You can't be a harmless bright light and attack others with your argumentative spirit. You can't be a pure and innocent bright light while contradicting everyone who does not think just like you. You can't be a bright light above reproach with your discontented, ungrateful pride! You can't be selfish like the world! How can the positive attitudes below change a once murmuring, complaining, argumentative heart into a pure, innocent, blameless, harmless, unselfish heart?

• Contentment

_____

• Forgiveness

_____

• Tolerance

_____

• Humility

_____

• Thankfulness

_____

"Lord, I am prone to be selfish and show it by a murmuring, argumentative spirit. I am selfish and I know it. Please help me change so I can be a bright testimony for You in this dark world."

Week 4: The attitude of an unselfish Christian.
Wednesday: Philippians 2:15b-18

The unselfish attitude of a joyful servant

Among whom ye shine as lights in the world; holding forth the word of life; that I may rejoice in the day of Christ, that I have not run in vain, neither laboured in vain. Yea, and if I be offered upon the sacrifice and service of your faith, I joy, and rejoice with you all. For the same cause also do ye joy, and rejoice with me.

Holding out for all to see (as a bright light in a dark world) **the Word of life,** so **that I may rejoice in the day of Christ, that I have not run in vain** (strenuously raced for nothing) or **laboured in vain** (toiled to the point of exhaustion for nothing). **And** yes, even **if I** am to be martyred, serving you by being poured out as a sacrificial drink offering **for your faith, I joy,** am glad, **and rejoice with all** of **you**. I beg you, **for the same** reason (your faith) you too should **also** be glad **and rejoice with me** by sharing your joy with me.

1. Selfish people do only that which is best for themselves. If it does not make their life better or easier, they are not going there. "What's in it for me?" seems to be a foundational question when it comes to serving today. What a difference from the way Paul viewed life, especially his life. Carefully read Philippians 2:16-18 again. Basically Paul was saying, "I may never get out of this prison alive. I may be poured out as a sacrificial offering. If I give my life for you, and if I die for you, I REJOICE!" Most of us are not willing to die for others. God may not ask you to die, but He would be pleased if you would simply live for others. Ministries all over our country (and the world) are in desperate need of full-time, vocational Christian workers. If you are prone to ask, "What's in it for me?" you will probably not consider such a life of ministry. If you can find true outrageous, contagious joy in serving others, then full-time, vocational ministry may be the way you should direct your life's focus. For each one of the occupations below, describe some sacrifices and some joys of such a lifestyle.

• Pastor of a local church

_____

• Christian school teacher

_____

• Local church music pastor

_____

• Foreign missionary

_____

• Christian camp worker

_____

• Church secretary

_____

• Christian college professor

_____

• Christian school coach/administrator

2. **Among whom ye shine as lights in the world; holding forth the word of life.**

We live in a dark world. Although many are scared of the dark, many others love the darkness over the light so that no one can see their sinfulness. Our selfish wickedness is made painfully clear by the Word of God as it is proclaimed through the lives of bright, vibrant, unselfish Christians. The **word of life** specifically refers to the gospel of Jesus Christ. The gospel offends some and comforts others. At one point, Jesus offended many (driving them away) as He shared the words of life. Jesus then asked His twelve apostles, "Will you also go away?" Read John 6:67-69 and give Simon Peter's answer to the Lord's question. Have you answered in the same way?

3. **That I may rejoice in the day of Christ, that I have not run in vain** or **laboured in vain.** Paul looked forward to the day of Christ with confidence knowing that he could never be accused of being lazy, apathetic, or complacent. He "ran" and he **laboured**. He ran in such a way that every spiritual muscle in his body was stretched and strained to the point of exhaustion. He labored until his strength was depleted. He did not quit. He did not tire. He did not give up because the pressure was too great. He was confident that he would someday **rejoice** in the very presence of Jesus Christ. He ran and labored with absolutely no regrets. Are you on the verge of giving up? In what way do you struggle with apathy or laziness in the normal disciplines of the Christian life (reading, praying, serving, obeying)? Will you be able to stand before God with no regrets **in the day of Christ**?

4. **Yea, and if I be offered upon the sacrifice and service of your faith.** Paul was actually saying, "I may never get out of this situation alive. I may be poured out as a libation (an act that pagan worshippers did with their chalice of wine before or after a meal either to gain favor or soften the anger of their gods). If I give my life for you and if I die for you, I JOY and REJOICE!" Most of us have never had to sacrifice for the cause of Christ. Paul gave up comfort, prestige, and now possibly his life in order to serve Christ. Name the greatest sacrifice you personally have made for God.

5. **I joy, and rejoice with you all. For the same cause also do ye joy, and rejoice with me.** This is **joy** on purpose. Paul's **joy** was not based on comfort or convenience but was based on the accomplishment of his mission in life—that Jesus Christ's death, burial, and resurrection be preached for all to hear. Have you ever experienced the joy of seeing a friend saved or a young Christian brother gaining victory over a sinful habit? What do you need to do to experience such **joy**?

"Lord, I don't think I could be as optimistic about dying as Paul was. Please give me such a love for You and others that I would be willing to die for both You and them."

WEEK 4: THE ATTITUDE OF AN UNSELFISH CHRISTIAN.
THURSDAY: PHILIPPIANS 2:19-24

THE UNSELFISH ATTITUDE OF A SINCERE FRIEND: TIMOTHY

But I trust in the Lord Jesus to send Timotheus shortly unto you, that I also may be of good comfort, when I know your state. For I have no man likeminded, who will naturally care for your state. For all seek their own, not the things which are Jesus Christ's. But ye know the proof of him, that, as a son with the father, he hath served with me in the gospel. Him therefore I hope to send presently, so soon as I shall see how it will go with me. But I trust in the Lord that I also myself shall come shortly.

But I trust in the Lord Jesus to send Timotheus (one of my very best friends) **shortly unto you, that I also may be of good comfort** (encouraged), **when I know your state** (condition). **For I have no man likeminded** (no one with such a kindred spirit), **who will naturally care** (be genuinely concerned) **for your state** (your good, your well-being). **For all seek their own** (their own interests, their own selfish pursuits), **not the things which are Jesus Christ's** (not the interests of our Lord). **But ye know the proof of him, that, as a son with the father, he hath served with me in the gospel** (he has proven himself that he is not like this unselfish, lazy, griping, complaining world, but genuinely, honestly, and unselfishly wants what is best for you). **Him therefore I hope to send presently, so soon as I shall see how it will go with me** (whether I am going to die in this prison). **But I trust in the Lord** (I am confident) **that I also myself shall come shortly.**

1. The joy of having the right kind of friends is almost impossible to describe. It is a joy to know that there is someone who cares more about you than they do for themselves. Those "kindred spirits" are like-souled friends who live in your own head and can almost read your motives. Solomon has much to say about true, like-souled friends that bring outrageous, contagious joy. Finish these verses:

• Proverbs 17:17 **A friend loveth** _____

_____

• Proverbs 27:6 **Faithful are the** _____

_____

• Proverbs 27:9 **Ointment and perfume rejoice the heart** _____

_____

• Proverbs 27:17 **Iron sharpeneth iron** _____

_____

2. Even though the Philippian believers knew of Timothy, Paul wanted to reintroduce him to their young church. Paul's formal introduction of his ministry friend described a guy that most of us would love to imitate. By the time we are done with this study, we will all wish that our pastors could say the same things about us that Paul said about Timothy. In what ways do you already imitate Paul's friend Timothy?

_____

_____

3. Timothy was an encourager **(that I also may be of good comfort)**. This guy knew how to comfort a hurting heart. The word **comfort** comes from two words meaning "well-souled" or "good-minded." It describes a guy who encourages others to think well, to think purely in an impure world, to think positively in a negative world, to think unselfishly in a self-centered world. We often think like those we hang out with. Do you have friends who encourage you to think in a way that pleases God? In what way do you (or should you) encourage your friends to think positively, purely, and unselfishly?

_____

_____

4. Timothy was a kindred spirit **(For I have no man likeminded)**. Timothy's heart and Paul's heart desired the same things. Timothy and Paul were **likeminded**, like-souled, like-desired friends. This kind of friend only comes once or twice in a lifetime. The more we are **likeminded** with Christ and Scripture, the more chance we will have to find a friend with such a kindred spirit. (If you are not sure what a kindred spirit is, ask an *Anne of Green Gables* addict.) Paul and Timothy obviously attempted to follow the admonition from Philippians 2:5, **Let this mind be in you which was also in Christ Jesus**. If Paul and Timothy lived today, would you be able to be one of their **likeminded** friends? Why or why not?

_____

_____

5. Timothy genuinely cared **(who will naturally care for your state)**. Timothy's concern for others was obvious. He cared! His care was not hypocritical, fake, or manufactured but was as natural to him as breathing. Great care for others presupposes little care for yourself. He may have learned it from his godly mother and grandmother or simply allowed the Spirit of God to so work in his heart that it mirrored what is said of God in 1 Peter 5:7, **Casting all your care on Him: for He careth for you.** The word used for **care** in our text has the concept of active concern (even anxious, troubled thought). Timothy took time to think about those God had called him to serve. He forsook his own thoughts (which today would probably be connected to a cell phone or an iPod) long enough to be genuinely concerned for others. How could you "up" your commitment to care for others and God more than you do now?

_____

_____

6. Timothy was an unselfish servant **(all seek their own, not the things which are Jesus Christ's… he served with me in the gospel)**. Timothy did not seem to be concerned about himself but unselfishly served others by desiring for them the same things that Christ desired for them. The word **seek** in our text gives the idea of longing for or striving to find. It is not a casual glance, but a determined look. Look for ways to be a like-minded, caring, unselfish servant like Timothy. In what way do you actively look for ways to draw others to Christ?

_____

_____

"Lord, I want to be a friend like Timothy. Help me to be a like-minded, caring, unselfish encourager like Paul's dear friend, Timothy."

WEEK 4: THE ATTITUDE OF AN UNSELFISH CHRISTIAN.
FRIDAY: PHILIPPIANS 2:25-30

THE UNSELFISH ATTITUDE OF A SELFLESS SERVANT: EPAPHRODITUS

Yet I supposed it necessary to send to you Epaphroditus, my brother, and companion in labor, and fellowsoldier, but your messenger, and he that ministered to my wants. For he longed after you all, and was full of heaviness, because that ye had heard that he had been sick. For indeed he was sick nigh unto death: but God had mercy on him; and not on him only, but on me also, lest I should have sorrow upon sorrow. I sent him therefore the more carefully, that, when ye see him again, ye may rejoice, and that I may be the less sorrowful. Receive him therefore in the Lord with all gladness; and hold such in reputation: because for the work of Christ he was nigh unto death, not regarding his life, to supply your lack of service toward me.

[But, I do have another friend very much like Timothy!] **Yet I supposed it necessary to send to you Epaphroditus, my brother, and companion in labor, and fellowsoldier, but your messenger, and he that ministered to my wants** (this guy was a true servant). **For he longed after you all, and was full of heaviness, because that ye had heard that he had been sick** (this guy really cared). **For indeed he was sick nigh unto death: but God had mercy on him; and not on him only, but on me also, lest I should have sorrow upon sorrow** (I don't know what I would do if I lost such an unselfish friend). **I sent him therefore the more carefully** (eagerly), **that, when ye see him again, ye may rejoice, and that I may be the less sorrowful** (less concerned and worried about you [I know, I'm not supposed to worry!]). **Receive him therefore in the Lord with all gladness; and hold such in reputation** (honor men like Epaphroditus): **because for the work of Christ he was nigh unto death, not regarding his life** (he did not seem to care if he died or not—of course, we've been meditating together on that "heaven-being-far-better" truth), **to supply your lack of service toward me** (to do for me what you wish you could do but were too far away).

Paul's second, life-impacting friend was Epaphroditus. God inspired Paul to write a short 140-word paragraph on this unusually selfless individual. If one of your closest friends were asked to write a short paragraph on your life, what would they say? Don't you hope that they would describe you like Paul described Epaphroditus? (You have to wonder if Paul gave Epaphroditus a nickname so he didn't have to say his entire name--Big E, Pap, Aphro, Ditus--your guess is as good as mine.) Let's study his life.

1. Epaphroditus was Paul's brother in the Lord **(Epaphroditus, my brother)**. Men can gather dozens of degrees and tons of titles such as Doctor, Reverend, or Professor, but none have a warmer and more satisfying sound than **brother**. Being part of God's family gives us the joy of gaining many new brothers and sisters in Christ. List three "brothers or sisters" that have encouraged your heart in the Lord.

---

2. Epaphroditus was a faithful **companion**. The key word behind companion is the word "with." A faithful companion will serve with, will suffer with, will laugh with, and will cry with. Epaphroditus was like superglue! He stuck with Paul during the good and the bad. He was with Paul as a

preacher and a prisoner. Paul could count on Epaphroditus to be there. In what two ways did Paul describe Epaphroditus to his friends at Colosse (Colossians 1:7-8)?

_____

_____

3. Epaphroditus was one of the hardest workers Paul knew **(companion in labor)**. Work. Work. Work. Do you dread it or delight in it? We know that hard work was not part of the curse (as some teenagers would argue) because Adam worked in the garden before the fall. When Paul called Epaphroditus a companion in labor, he simply meant that Epaphroditus was willing to sweat, toil, and get tired working hard. Too many today are afraid of hard work. Life was not meant to be a year-round vacation where we can laze around playing computer games and watching movies all day. God set up an example to work hard for six days and rest for one. Some of us get that equation switched around. In what way do you "work hard" each day? (If you can't think of something, explain how you should work hard each day.)

_____

_____

4. Epaphroditus will fight for those he loves and serves **(fellowsoldier)**. Epaphroditus was a fighter. Not only could he have been called a fellow worker (*sunergos*) but also a **fellowsoldier** (*sustratiotes*). The prefix *su* or *sun* means "with." Not only was he willing to work alongside of (with) Paul but also to fight (be willing to die) alongside of (with) Paul. Talk about a true friend! Most conveniently end their friendships when things get wearisome, unpopular, or difficult. Epaphroditus was the kind of friend that was "with" Paul when he was preaching or in prison. Do you stick up for your Christian friends at work or at school? Are you willing to defend them when they are mocked or ridiculed? A **fellowsoldier** would. List three of your friends who would stick with you and defend you even if it meant a fight.

_____

_____

5. Epaphroditus was a true servant **(He that ministered to my wants. For he longed after you all, and was full of heaviness, because that ye had heard that he had been sick. For indeed he was sick nigh unto death)**. Epaphroditus almost worked himself to the grave. He refused to slow down! Do you know anyone like that? Would anyone say that you were that kind of servant? We need to take care of ourselves, but we should also be willing to serve until we are exhausted. True servants do not focus on their own schedules, hours, or weariness, but keep their focus on God and others. Paul knew if he ever lost Epaphroditus as a friend, his heart would break. This is why he mentions having **sorrow upon sorrow**. From our study today, in what way are you the most like Epaphroditus and why?

_____

_____

"Lord, help me to be the same kind of example to my friends as Paul's friend Epaphroditus was to him. Help me to be a committed worker, soldier, and servant just like Epaphroditus."

Saturday & Sunday
Review
Philippians 2:12-30

What did Philippians 2:12-13 teach you about the unselfish attitude of an obedient believer?

What did Philippians 2:14-15 teach you about the unselfish attitude of a blameless child?

What did Philippians 2:15b-18 teach you about the unselfish attitude of a joyful servant?

_____
_____
_____
_____
_____
_____
_____
_____
_____
_____

What did Philippians 2:19-24 teach you about the unselfish attitude of a sincere friend like Timothy?

_____
_____
_____
_____
_____
_____
_____
_____
_____
_____

What did Philippians 2:25-30 teach you about the attitude of a selfless servant like Epaphroditus?

_____
_____
_____
_____
_____
_____
_____
_____
_____
_____

Principle Three:

An Eternal Focus Produces Outrageous Joy!

Philippians 3:1-21

Week 5: An eternal focus.

Monday: Philippians 3:1-6

Never focus on your past accomplishments–Part 1

Finally, my brethren, rejoice in the Lord. To write the same things to you, to me indeed is not grievous, but for you it is safe. Beware of dogs, beware of evil workers, beware of the concision. For we are the circumcision, which worship God in the spirit, and rejoice in Christ Jesus, and have no confidence in the flesh. Though I might also have confidence in the flesh. If any other man thinketh that he hath whereof he might trust in the flesh, I more: circumcised the eighth day, of the stock of Israel, of the tribe of Benjamin, an Hebrew of the Hebrews; as touching the law, a Pharisee; concerning zeal, persecuting the church; touching the righteousness which is in the law, blameless.

Finally, my brethren, rejoice in the Lord. To write the same things (over and over) **to you, to me indeed is not grievous** (really, it is no trouble at all, it is not tedious or tiresome when I know how it will benefit you), **but for you it is safe** (it is a safeguard; it is something secure and stable; it is the absolute truth that you can put your confidence in). **Beware of** the **dogs** (watch out for unclean scavengers who feed on those they can pull away from the absolute truth of God), **beware of** the **evil workers** (wicked and vicious in character), **beware of the concision** (the false circumcision more concerned with outward show than inward character). **For we are the** (true) **circumcision** (true believers), who **worship God in the Spirit, and rejoice in Christ Jesus, and have** (put) **no confidence in the flesh**, although **I might have confidence** (reasons to boast) **in the flesh. If** anyone else thinks he has a right to **trust** (put confidence) **in the flesh, I** have much **more** right than they: **circumcised the eighth day, of the stock** (nation) **of Israel, of the tribe of Benjamin,** a **Hebrew of Hebrews; as touching the law, a Pharisee; concerning zeal**, I personally became a persecutor of **the church**; as to **the** (legalistic) **righteousness which is in the law**, I was found faultless and **blameless.**

1. One Bible commentator referred to Paul as a spiritual accountant. Accountants have the ability to put on paper the true value or worth of an estate or an individual. Paul did his own audit and found out one simple truth: "I am nothing. I deserve nothing. I have never been anything. Any good that comes to me after this life is from the kind, gracious, hand of God." In the first six verses of this chapter Paul warns us against listening to the wrong kind of "accounting firms" by using the word **beware** three times. If the three "bewares" were made into yard signs, what would they say?

- _____
- _____
- _____

Paul is not just name-calling as he describes these false teachers as **dogs**, **evil workers**, and the **concision**, but is actually describing what they do to turn individuals away from God. When God tells us to "beware," we had better listen!

• **Beware of dogs.** Some dogs are vicious and should be avoided. So are false teachers who teach salvation by works. Watch out for those unclean, yapping scavengers who feed on those they can pull away from the absolute truth of God with their prideful false teaching.

• **Beware of evil workers.** Many pretending to be working for God are actually evil phonies and wicked imposters attacking anything or anyone good.

- **Beware of the concision.** Paul calls these false Jewish teachers **concision** because while teaching that outward circumcision of the flesh was necessary to salvation, their hearts were consumed with pride and wickedness.

2. Salvation is a free gift received by faith to those who believe. If anyone was good enough to earn favor with God, it was Paul. Paul clearly explains that all the "good" that he had done could in no way earn his salvation. Paul reminded the Philippians in verses 4-6 that salvation was not by ritual, race, tradition, religion, sincerity, or legalistic righteousness. According to Philippians 3:7, how did Paul view all these accomplishments?

_____

Consider our world today with the teachings of cults and the ever-increasing popularity of the Muslim religion and explain why Paul attacked the false teachers.

_____
_____

3. True believers (what Paul called **the circumcision**) will be known for three things.

- True believers **worship God in the Spirit**. God saved believers to worship Him. Write out the last phrase of John 4:23.

_____
_____

Write out Psalm 95:6 which seems to express much of what Scripture has to say about worship.

_____
_____

In our day of "praise and worship" services, bands, and leaders, we forget that we should be humbled and bow down to worship before we ever stand to praise. In what way do some "praise and worship" services violate this truth?

_____
_____
_____

- True believers **rejoice in Christ Jesus** and what He has done for them. Our salvation is all of God. It is not us! We are wicked. We cannot attain salvation by our own efforts, goodness, kindness, or work. Therefore, we must give credit to the Lord Jesus Christ. With Paul we must declare, **By the grace of God I am what I am.** When was the last time you thanked God personally or publicly for your salvation? _____

- True believers put **no confidence in the flesh** (what they have done) for salvation. Paul declared that all his religious accomplishments meant absolutely nothing! His race and rank, his traditions and rituals, his sincerity were all rubbish. The only thing that matters both now and for eternity is knowing Christ! What are some of the excellent, surpassing benefits of knowing Christ as Savior and Lord?

_____
_____

"Lord, help me keep my focus off myself and my feeble accomplishments in life. Help me focus on You and my heavenly home. Thank you for saving me!"

WEEK 5: AN ETERNAL FOCUS.
TUESDAY: PHILIPPIANS 3:7-11

NEVER FOCUS ON YOUR PAST ACCOMPLISHMENTS–PART 2

But what things were gain to me, those I counted loss for Christ. Yea doubtless, and I count all things but loss for the excellency of the knowledge of Christ Jesus my Lord: for whom I have suffered the loss of all things, and do count them but dung, that I may win Christ, and be found in Him, not having mine own righteousness, which is of the law, but that which is through the faith of Christ, the righteousness which is of God by faith: that I may know Him, and the power of His resurrection, and the fellowship of His sufferings, being made conformable unto His death; if by any means I might attain unto the resurrection of the dead.

But what things were gain or profit **to me, those I counted** and considered **loss for Christ.** Without a doubt, **and I count** (consider) **all things but loss** compared to **the excellency** (surpassing value) of personally knowing **(the knowledge)** Christ Jesus my Lord: **for whom I have suffered the loss of all things, and do** consider **them but** rubbish and trash, **that I may win Christ** (gain Christ), **and be found in Him, not having mine own righteousness, which is of the law** (not a personal righteousness that I have achieved by keeping rules and regulations), **but that which is through the faith of Christ, the righteousness** that comes from God and is **by faith: that I may know Him, and the power of His resurrection, and the fellowship of His sufferings** (Paul wanted to experience firsthand the power to overcome sin and was willing to suffer like Christ to experience such power), **being made conformable unto His death; if by any means I might attain unto the resurrection of the dead** (someday I will understand all that I have in Christ when I am resurrected from the dead and am in heaven with Christ).

1. Paul was reminding the Philippian believers of the far-surpassing value of what they gained by having a personal relationship with Christ rather than by living by a strict adherence to the law: knowledge, righteousness, power, fellowship, and glory.

KNOWLEDGE

I count all things but loss for the excellency of the knowledge of Christ Jesus my Lord: Knowing Christ as my personal Savior far surpasses any and all accomplishments in my life. The **excellency**, the far surpassing greatness, the superior value of knowing the truth that I could not earn God's favor by being good (keeping the law) but that Christ did everything necessary for my sins to be forgiven. Because of this great knowledge, Paul said, **I count.** Paul knew how to count. (Do you remember when you learned to count to a hundred? By ones! By tens! You were probably in preschool and were excited about sharing your great "counting ability" with anyone who would listen, much like Paul is doing here in the spiritual realm.) **Count** (*hegeomai*), which Paul uses twice in this one sentence, actually means to put first in your thinking, to view, regard, esteem, or honestly value. "Counted" is in the perfect tense and **count** is in the present tense which in practical terms means, anything I counted on in the past and anything I might count on in the future to earn God's favor is worthless. In one word, how important is your salvation to you?

RIGHTEOUSNESS

Not having mine own righteousness, which is of the law, but that which is through the faith of Christ, the righteousness which is of God by faith: Paul is saying, I am truly righteous, but not because of anything I have done, for I could never be good enough to earn God's favor, but because God chose to give it to me when I by faith put my trust in Him. Everything is "right" between me and God! How should that affect my assurance of salvation?

_____
_____

How should that affect my prayer life according to James 5:16?

_____
_____

POWER

That I may know Him, and the power of His resurrection: Most of us are content to live powerless lives—not Paul. He desired to experience the same **power** in his daily walk with Christ that was displayed by Christ when Christ defeated death and rose from the grave. This power saves us from the penalty of sin of the past, strengthens us against the power of sin in the present, and will secure us from the presence of sin in the future. It is not that the power is not available, we simply are either too distracted, too busy, too lazy, or too selfish to accept it. What do the following verses promise us because Christ dwells within our hearts?

- Ephesians 6:10 _____
- Philippians 4:13 _____
- Colossians 1:11 _____

FELLOWSHIP

And the fellowship of His sufferings, being made conformable unto His death: Paul was not a stranger to suffering (neither was Jesus). When you share your burdens, heartaches, and sufferings with someone who has been there before and experienced the same hurt, your hearts are quickly cemented together because you understand each other's hearts. That's fellowship. The word **fellowship** (_koinonia_) actually gives the idea of a close, intimate communion based on a mutual understanding. Take your suffering (the times you have been laughed at, mocked, ridiculed, and misunderstood) and compare it with what our Lord experienced the week of His death and your suffering pales in comparison. List one way that you and Jesus Christ experienced similar hate, rejection, or ridicule and then explain the way that Christ handled the suffering and how you are presently dealing with it.

_____
_____

GLORY

If by any means I might attain unto the resurrection of the dead: Paul was assured of his resurrection from the dead when he would be "with" Christ forever sharing in His glory. Christian, you and I will experience the same. Amen and amen!

"Lord, thank You. Thank You for everything that You have given me! My spiritual knowledge, righteousness, power, fellowship, and glory is all from You. Thank You, Lord."

Week 5: An eternal focus.
Wednesday: Philippians 3:12-16

Never focus on your present accomplishments

Not as though I had already attained, either were already perfect: but I follow after, if that I may apprehend that for which also I am apprehended of Christ Jesus. Brethren, I count not myself to have apprehended: but this one thing I do, forgetting those things which are behind, and reaching forth unto those things which are before, I press toward the mark for the prize of the high calling of God in Christ Jesus. Let us therefore, as many as be perfect, be thus minded: and if in any thing ye be otherwise minded, God shall reveal even this unto you. Nevertheless, whereto we have already attained, let us walk by the same rule, let us mind the same thing.

Not as though I had already attained (I have a long way to go), **either were already perfect** (Maturity is my goal but I do struggle with immaturity): **but I follow after** (I press on; I keep trying; I don't quit even when it hurts; I keep running even when I'm exhausted), **if that I may apprehend that for which also I am apprehended of Christ Jesus.** (My goal in life is the same goal that God had for saving me: to be conformed to the image of His Son, or simply stated, Christlikeness.) **Brethren, I count not myself to have apprehended: but this one thing I do** (I'm not there, but here is what I am going to spend the rest of my life doing), **forgetting those things which are behind, and reaching forth unto those things which are before, I press toward the mark for the prize of the high calling of God in Christ Jesus.** (I refuse to focus on my past failures or my past accomplishments. I refuse to apathetically sit around and wait for something to happen. I will run, wrestle, and fight my way to spiritual maturity. I will strive to be like Christ.) **Let us** (I am not in this alone as we all need to have this desire and goal) **therefore, as many as be perfect, be thus minded** (those who have reached some level of spiritual maturity should agree with what I am saying): **and if in any thing ye be otherwise minded, God shall reveal even this unto you.** (those who refuse to see this, God will correct through His Word, His Spirit, or chastening.) **Nevertheless, whereto we have already attained, let us walk by the same rule, let us mind the same thing.** (However, let us at least live up to the degree of maturity we have already attained.)

1. Paul knew the discipline and mind-set of an Olympic athlete when he said in verse 14, **I press toward the mark for the prize of the high calling of God in Christ Jesus.** Even for today's Olympian, the "gold" is all they want. It is what they live for. It consumes their childhood and controls their teen years. Paul exhibited that same kind of desire and drive in his spiritual life. Can you say the same? In what way do you approach your Christian life with the intensity and discipline of an Olympic marathon runner?

_____

_____

There is comfort in our text today as Paul explained that even after thirty years as a Christian, he still had not arrived. He never said that he "won" the race; he said that he "ran" the race. For a second time, read the meditation of Philippians 3:12-16 above and write both two convicting principles and two comforting principles that could affect your walk with God today.

_____

_____

_____

2. Compiling our thoughts from the last three days of meditation and study in the first sixteen verses of Philippians 3, Paul is simply and honestly saying,

> "I am nothing. I deserve nothing. I have never been anything. Any good that comes to me after this life is from the kind, gracious, hand of God."

Aside from what God has done for me I have nothing to smile about. Aside from what God is doing through me I have nothing to find joy in. Aside from what God will do for me in eternity it is impossible to experience outrageous, contagious joy. It is all of God. For this simple reason alone I need to run, fight, and willingly offer my life and strength for God's eternal glory. I must keep growing. I must keep fighting. I must keep wrestling with the enemies of life to do all I can to further the cause of Christ. What enemies are you currently wrestling with that hinder your walk with God?

_____

_____

3. **Let us therefore, as many as be perfect, be thus minded: and if in any thing ye be otherwise minded, God shall reveal even this unto you**. When Paul said **us** he was expressing the truth that we are not in this alone. We must encourage each other to keep in the forefront of our minds the commitment to keep running, to keep wrestling, and to refuse to quit. Then he said, if you **be otherwise minded**, or, if you have already changed your mind about living for God and are ready to quit, God will show you where you are wrong either through His Word or by a biblically based friend. Who in your church, school, or family is about to quit on God? What have you learned today about pressing on that you could share with those **otherwise minded** quitters?

_____

_____

_____

4. **Nevertheless, whereto we have already attained, let us walk by the same rule, let us mind the same thing**. However, let us at least live up to the degree of maturity we have already attained. Carefully evaluate what you were like five years ago and what you are like now. Have you changed? Have you matured? In what areas of temptation have you been victorious so many times it is no longer a struggle in your life? Now, some have slipped and slid through their walk with God and have not grown...that is not God's fault. In the last five years, how have you grown in your...

• prayer life? _____

• personal Bible study? _____

• faithfulness in church? _____

Now, don't be content with your growth, but keep growing in the grace of God! Amen.

"Lord, help me to never be a quitter. Encourage my heart to keep running, fighting, and wrestling with the issues of life that hinder me. Help me to keep growing in You."

Week 5: An eternal focus.

Thursday: Philippians 3:17-19

Focus on the accomplishments of Christlike leaders

Brethren, be followers together of me, and mark them which walk so as ye have us for an ensample. (For many walk, of whom I have told you often, and now tell you even weeping, that they are the enemies of the cross of Christ: whose end is destruction, whose god is their belly, and whose glory is in their shame, who mind earthly things.)

Brethren, be followers together of me, and mark them which walk so as ye have us for an ensample. (Join with others in following my example, brothers, and mark, take note, keep your eye on those godly friends and influences who live according to the example and pattern that Timothy, Epaphroditus, and I have set for you.) **For many walk** (There are many enemies of the cross of Christ who walk all around you. If, by the way, you keep Christ as your focus, don't plan on being popular. There are many who will disagree with you.), **of whom I have told you often** (I have warned you many times), **and now tell you even weeping** (It breaks my heart! I hate that there are so many who will attempt to turn your focus off Christ and what He has done for you. Let me explain the consequences of those who proudly say that their way of earning God's favor is better.): **whose end is destruction** (their destiny is eternal destruction in hell), **whose god is their belly** (their fleshly appetites have become the gods who they serve and worship), **whose glory is in their shame** (Their only accomplishments worthy of bragging rights or boasting is the extent of their shameful wickedness, immorality, and rebellion. They actually brag that they have defied God.), **who mind earthly things** (their minds are consumed with the here and now).

1. Most of us have had the unique experience of playing the childhood game of "Follow the Leader" by skipping, running, twisting, or rolling across a playground. Paul carefully encouraged these young believers to be careful which "leader" they were going to follow. There were some to **mark** (take note of) and follow and others to **mark** (keep their eyes on) and flee. Just because someone is a leader does not mean that they are willing to lead in the right direction. If we are not careful who we follow, we can be led into sin just as easily as we can be led into righteousness. Philippians 3:17 focuses on the right kind of leaders while verses 18-19 focus on the wrong kind of leaders. Before we look closely at both, list three leaders in your life and comment on how and where they are leading you.

_____

_____

_____

2. **Brethren, be followers together of me, and mark them which walk so as ye have us for an ensample.** Paul was reminding the Philippians to join with others in following his example and to take note of those godly friends and influences who live according to the example and pattern left by Timothy, Epaphroditus, and Paul. Refer back to last week's Thursday and Friday studies of Philippians 2:19-30 to reacquaint yourselves with Paul's two "iron sharpening" friends and then list the unique characteristics both friends had that gave them the influence on Paul that they had.

Paul's friend Timothy (Philippians 2:19-24) _____

_____

Paul's friend Epaphroditus (Philippians 2:25-30) _____

_____

If Paul was writing this epistle today and referring to your church, how many can you think of in your church or youth group that could be examples to other believers in their walk with God? List the names of two individuals you consider good, godly examples to follow.

_____

Do you think that any of your friends would have put your name down for that question? Why or why not?

_____

3. **For many walk, of whom I have told you often, and now tell you even weeping, that they are the enemies of the cross of Christ: whose end is destruction, whose god is their belly, and whose glory is in their shame, who mind earthly things.** Living for God in a selfish world is not the popular thing to do. Paul's heart was literally broken as he was stirred to tears when he thought about those who were sacrificing their futures in order to experience the pleasures of satisfying their flesh. We tend to criticize others rather than cry for them. Paul's broken heart verbalized the consequences of their sin. Fill in the Bible phrase that matches the following consequences. Who in your circle of influence needs to understand these facts from a caring, broken-hearted friend?

• Their destiny was eternal destruction in hell.
_____

• Their fleshly appetites became the gods they served, worshiped, and lived for.
_____

• The only accomplishments worthy of bragging rights was the extent of their shameful wickedness, immorality, and rebellion.
_____

• Their minds were consumed with the "here and now" of their day. All they had to look forward to were the simple joys they manufactured in their short life and now all they have for eternity are the memories of their shameful, earthly existence.
_____

What would keep you from being that kind of friend?
_____

"Lord, I want to be a godly friend like Timothy, an encouraging brother like Epaphroditus, and a motivating leader like Paul. Also, Lord, please break my heart for unbelievers."

PRINCIPLE THREE: AN ETERNAL FOCUS PRODUCES OUTRAGEOUS JOY!

WEEK 5: AN ETERNAL FOCUS.
FRIDAY: PHILIPPIANS 3:20-21

FOCUS ON THE ETERNAL ACCOMPLISHMENTS OF CHRIST

For our conversation is in heaven; from whence also we look for the Savior, the Lord Jesus Christ: Who shall change our vile body, that it may be fashioned like unto His glorious body, according to the working whereby He is able even to subdue all things unto Himself.

For our conversation (our citizenship) **is in heaven; from whence also we look** (we eagerly long for and wait) **for the Savior, the Lord Jesus Christ:** Who **according to the working** (by the enabling power) **by which He is able even to subdue all things to Himself** (the power that brings everything under His mighty control) **will change** (totally transform) **our vile** (humiliating, sinful, lowly) **body that it may be fashioned** (conformed) **to His glorious** (resurrected) **body.**

1. Paul explained that his **conversation** (which here simply means "citizenship") **is in heaven** and that he did not belong on this earth. He was a stranger, a pilgrim, an alien. Those of you who know Christ as your Savior could consider yourselves spiritual aliens. (You are spiritual creatures from outer space and some of you have the looks to go with it.) I don't think Paul was thinking of outer space creatures when he used the word **alien** in Ephesians 2:12, but simply meant strangers or people from a different part of the world. What do the following passages say about the first phrase of the old gospel song, "This world is not my home, I'm just a passin' through"?

• **Dearly beloved, I beseech you as strangers and pilgrims, abstain from fleshly lusts, which war against the soul** (1 Peter 2:11).

_____
_____

• **For we know that if our earthly house of this tabernacle were dissolved, we have a building of God, an house not made with hands, eternal in the heavens** (2 Corinthians 5:1).

_____
_____

• **Love not the world, neither the things that are in the world. If any man love the world, the love of the Father is not in him. For all that is in the world, the lust of the flesh, and the lust of the eyes, and the pride of life, is not of the Father, but is of the world. And the world passeth away, and the lust thereof: but he that doeth the will of God abideth for ever** (1 John 2:15-17).

_____
_____

2. **From whence also we look for the Savior, the Lord Jesus Christ.** Do you want the Lord to return today? According to everything that is happening worldwide with the devastating storms, tsunamis, drought, floods, and unrest in the Middle East, it looks like the Lord may return this afternoon. Here are four meditative thoughts on the Lord's return that you could use to comfort your friends who are hoping that the Lord returns soon. List one characteristic of God that you see in each thought.

• As a joyful Bridegroom, Jesus is preparing a place for His bride.

_____

- As a loving Father, Jesus is patiently waiting for His children to repent.
___

- As a concerned Savior, Jesus is eagerly ready to rescue His loved ones from the dark, wicked world in which they live.
___

- As a sovereign King, Jesus is anticipating giving the command for the trumpets to sound to bring His nation and His family together…forever.
___

3. **Who shall change our vile body, that it may be fashioned like unto His glorious body.** How did Paul describe our earthly bodies?
___

In what way are our bodies going to be changed?
___
___

Do you think that our new, heavenly, eternal bodies will be tempted the same way that our vile, lowly bodies are on earth? Do you think we will tire or get weary in serving our Lord? List a couple of blessings that you might imagine a glorified body could enjoy.
___
___
___

The last phrase of this chapter, **according to the working whereby He is able even to subdue all things unto Himself**, simply means that Jesus Christ has the power that enables Him to place everything under His control. Everything! What a great God we serve. Nothing can stop God! Below is a word study for three words in this phrase--**working**, **able**, and **subdue**. Study each word and then try in your own words to explain this phrase in a way that a fourth grader could easily understand.

- **working** (*enérgeia*): active energy, active power at work
- **able** (*dúnamai*): to be able, to have the power to do, to be empowered
- **subdue** (*hupotássœ*): submission, to place under in an orderly fashion

___
___

4. Philippians 3:20-21 can quickly put joy in our hearts and a smile on our faces. Why would we NOT smile? God has the power and the energy to keep everything—everything in my past, everything in my present, and everything in my future—under His almighty, all-powerful control! This outrageous, contagious joy that Paul is discussing with the Philippians is not a result of our past or present accomplishments, but is based on what our Lord Jesus Christ has accomplished for us. Peter explained it this way, **For Christ…suffered for sins, the just for the unjust, that He might bring us to God** (1 Peter 3:18). Are you thankful for this?

"Lord, thank You for what You have done for me. You've made it possible for my sins to be forgiven. You've promised me a home in heaven. You brought me to God! Thank You!"

Saturday & Sunday
Review
Philippians 3:1-21

What did Philippians 3:1-6 teach you about your past accomplishments, an eternal focus, and outrageous joy?

_____
_____
_____
_____
_____
_____
_____
_____
_____
_____
_____

What did Philippians 3:7-11 teach you about your past accomplishments, an eternal focus, and outrageous joy?

_____
_____
_____
_____
_____
_____
_____
_____
_____
_____
_____

What did Philippians 3:12-16 teach you about your present accomplishments, an eternal focus, and outrageous joy?

What did Philippians 3:17-19 teach you about Christlike leaders, an eternal focus, and outrageous joy?

What did Philippians 3:20-21 teach you about Christ's accomplishments, an eternal focus, and outrageous joy?

Principle Four:

A Contented Heart Produces Contagious Joy!

Philippians 4:1-23

WEEK 6: A CONTENTED HEART.
MONDAY: PHILIPPIANS 4:1-3

CONTENTMENT COMES FROM AN UNDERSTANDING OF GOD'S PEOPLE

Therefore, my brethren dearly beloved and longed for, my joy and crown, so stand fast in the Lord, my dearly beloved. I beseech Euodias, and beseech Syntyche, that they be of the same mind in the Lord. And I intreat thee also, true yokefellow, help those women which labored with me in the gospel, with Clement also, and with other my fellowlaborers, whose names are in the book of life.

Therefore (because our citizenship is in heaven and not here on this selfish earth; because our vile bodies will be changed; because even though the world is against us, God is for us), **my brethren dearly beloved and longed for** (you know that I sincerely love you and earnestly desire to see you), **my joy** (you put a smile on my face just thinking about you) **and crown** (you make me very proud of you), **so stand fast in the Lord** (this is the second time I mentioned this, remember? [1:27] Before, I was talking about your enemies, now I'm talking about you! If you spend all your time fighting with each other, how will you have any time to fight your enemies?), **my dearly beloved.** (Oh, did I tell you that I loved you?) I beg (**beseech**) two of you ladies, **Euodias and Syntyche, that** you **be of the same mind in the Lord.** (You must learn to disagree agreeably.) And you, **my true** companion (**yokefellow**), **I also intreat** and beg you to **help those women which labored with me** and shared in my struggle, agonized with me in the cause of **the gospel**, you need to help them as does **Clement** and the rest of the church workers and leaders (**fellowlaborers**), **whose names are in the book of life.**

1. In our last chapter (and week) of study, Paul is emphasizing the necessity of contentment in your pursuit of real joy. Contentment is the realization that God has provided everything you need for your present happiness. Contentment is the eager acceptance and satisfaction in everything that God has orchestrated in your life. Discontentment with God is a root sin that will affect every relationship in your life. Think about how a discontented heart fights against what you have learned so far from Paul's letter to the Philippians.

Philippians 1: GOD-CONFIDENCE. Discontentment reveals a lack of confidence in God. "What if God messes up? What if God misses something? What if God makes a mistake?"

Philippians 2: UNSELFISH ATTITUDE. Discontentment reveals a prideful attitude. "I deserve more than I am getting. Doesn't God realize just how much I have accomplished for Him?"

Philippians 3: ETERNAL FOCUS. Discontentment reveals a temporal self-focus. Discontentment says, "I have a right to be bitter. God has been unfair to me. Everyone else has it so easy. Just look at the hardships I face every day. That's why I worry about the future. I fear that everything that could go wrong will go wrong."

Has discontentment crept into your heart? Of the three principles above, which one do you feel you struggle with the most and why?

_____

_____

2. Paul starts chapter four urging and begging two discontented ladies to get right with each other and the Lord. What were their names?

_____

It is obvious that they were having a problem with each other. These ladies labored with Paul in spreading the gospel and therefore had character. But their conflict could split their church and bring shame on the name of Christ. Who on this earth do you refuse to forgive? Is there anyone in your family, church, or school that you cannot get along with? Why?

_____

_____

Here are four good questions to ask yourself when you struggle getting along with someone in your family, church, school, or work.

1. What is your goal? (Do you insist on being right? Is your goal to win the argument?)

2. What is your motivation? (Do you both want the conflict resolved? Is your heart filled with malice? Are you purposely trying to hurt each other?)

3. What about your testimony? (What are your friends thinking? Are you making them take sides? Do they think you have lost your mind?)

4. What about your Lord? (How do you think the Lord sees your situation? What would He have done? How did He respond when others disagreed with Him? Would He be pleased with your attitude?)

Once again, who on this earth do you refuse to forgive? Is there anyone you cannot get along with? How would you answer the following questions?

1. What is your goal?

_____

2. What is your motivation?

_____

3. What about your testimony?

_____

4. What about your Lord?

_____

3. **And I intreat thee also, true yokefellow, help those women which labored with me in the gospel, with Clement also, and with other my fellowlaborers, whose names are in the book of life.** Here Paul is asking for help. He is asking Clement, a couple fellow workers, and some guy referred to as a **true yokefellow** to see what they could do. Obviously, Paul trusted these guys to help Euodias and Syntyche resolve their conflict. They were not to take sides or join in on the conflict but were to do everything they could to bring about reconciliation. Paul reminded them that they were all believers whose names were **in the book of life**. Is there anyone among your friends or family who hate each other and cannot get along? If Paul wrote to you and asked you to do something about their conflict, what would you do to help?

_____

_____

"Lord, You have given me a consuming, contagious joy. Help me to resolve all conflicts. Help me help others to resolve their conflicts so they too can experience the joy that You give. Amen."

WEEK 6: A CONTENTED HEART.

TUESDAY: PHILIPPIANS 4:4-6

CONTENTMENT COMES FROM AN UNDERSTANDING OF GOD'S PRESENCE

Rejoice in the Lord alway: and again I say, Rejoice. Let your moderation be known unto all men. The Lord is at hand. Be careful for nothing; but in every thing by prayer and supplication with thanksgiving let your requests be made known unto God.

Rejoice in the Lord alway. Let me say it **again, Rejoice! Let your moderation** (mild disposition or gentleness) **be known unto all men. The Lord is at hand** (His presence is so close it is as if you could almost reach out and touch Him). **Be careful** (anxious) **for nothing** (do not be full of care or full of worry), **but in everything by prayer and supplication with thanksgiving let your requests be made known unto God**.

1. Only a contented heart can rejoice in the Lord and live with a constant smile. Only a contented heart can be meek and gentle rather than harsh and vindictive. Only a contented heart can thank God for both the good and the bad that comes with life. Contentment is not based on circumstances, relationships, or success but on a proper view of God and God alone. Read Philippians 4:4-6 again and notice how our Lord's presence is an essential part of each of the three commands.

• If we are to always rejoice in the Lord, what does that say about God's presence?
_____

• If we are to be known for our gentle, mild disposition to all men, what phrase motivates us to do so?
_____

• If we are to share our requests with thanksgiving in prayer to God for everything whether it be day or night, what does that presuppose about God's listening ear?
_____

2. **Be careful for nothing** could be explained this way, "Don't be anxious, don't worry, and don't be troubled." Moms are not the only ones who can worry. Have you ever worried about whether or not you'll ever be married? Have you ever worried about your future? Have you ever worried about money for college? If you are not careful, you will be "full of care" about everything and won't be able to trust God. Jesus dealt with this same heart issue of worry (taking thought) in His "Sermon on the Mount" in Matthew 6. Jesus begins the message with the "beatitude attitude" that guarantees happiness for all participants. He then goes after the hypocrisy that seems to crawl into our giving, fasting, and praying. Jesus follows up with a huge need of His day (and ours)…worry. Turn to and read Matthew 6:25, 27, 28, 31, 34 and see what recurring words or phrase is mentioned in all five of these verses.
_____

This phrase, **be careful for nothing**, is sandwiched between two refocusing truths that are the enemies of worry. On the top we are told to rejoice. On the bottom we are told to be thankful. Explain clearly how those who **rejoice in the Lord** and make their requests in prayer to God **with thanksgiving** defeat the sin of worry?
_____
_____

3. **Let your moderation be known unto all men.** In our society, the joyful, mild-dispositioned, gentle-spirited man is becoming an endangered species. It is much more acceptable to be angry, harsh, and impatient. Road rage, school shootings, domestic violence, and terrorism mark our day. The word **moderation** is described in the following two verses. Describe a man of moderation from these verses.

• 1 Timothy 3:3

_____
_____
_____

• James 3:17

_____
_____
_____

4. **The Lord is at hand.** The Lord is near. How near? **At hand**! This could refer to either the Lord's presence or the Lord's return. Both are **at hand**. Read the following verses and state whether they refer to our Lord's presence or our Lord's return.

• James 5:8 **Be ye also patient; stablish your hearts: for the coming of the Lord draweth nigh.**
_____

• Psalm 34:18 **The LORD is nigh unto them that are of a broken heart; and saveth such as be of a contrite spirit.**
_____

• Hebrews 10:37 **For yet a little while, and He that shall come will come, and will not tarry.**
_____

• Psalm 119:151 **Thou art near, O LORD; and all Thy commandments are truth.**
_____

5. **By prayer and supplication with thanksgiving let your requests be made known to God.** Here Paul gives some practical advice about prayer. He used four words in this one phrase that should be part of our daily conversations with God. Prayer is talking to God, not to others about God, but to God. God is never too busy to talk to us. God loves for His children to cry out to Him for help and advice. God loves for us to pray to Him. Do you? Study each word below and use the thoughts to explain prayer in a way that a second grader could clearly understand how to pray.

• **prayer** (*proseuche*): prayer (wish) addressed to God, talking to God

• **supplication** (*deesis*): to make known a personal need or want

• **thanksgiving** (*eucharistia*): grateful, well pleasing, gratitude, thankful

• **requests** (*aitema*): to ask, petition, request a specific need or want

_____
_____

"Lord, I don't want to worry. Help me be a kind, gentle, rejoicing, praying, thankful believer. Help me be so in tune with Your presence that it controls my every thought."

Week 6: A contented heart.
Wednesday: Philippians 4:7-9

Contentment comes from an understanding of God's peace

And the peace of God, which passeth all understanding, shall keep your hearts and minds through Christ Jesus. Finally, brethren, whatsoever things are true, whatsoever things are honest, whatsoever things are just, whatsoever things are pure, whatsoever things are lovely, whatsoever things are of good report; if there be any virtue, and if there be any praise, think on these things. Those things, which ye have both learned, and received, and heard, and seen in me, do: and the God of peace shall be with you.

And the peace of God, which passeth all understanding (comprehension), will **keep** (guard like a soldier) **your hearts and minds** (the real you) in **Christ Jesus. Finally, brethren,** whatever is **true**, whatever is **honest** (honorable), whatever is **just** (right, fair), whatever is **pure** (free from defilement), whatever is **lovely**, whatever is of **good report** (admirable, of good repute); **if there is any virtue** (moral excellence), **and if** anything worthy of **praise**, **think** (let your mind dwell) **on these things**. The **things you have learned, and received, and heard, and seen in me, do** (imitate these things): **and the God of peace** will **be with you**.

1. **And the peace of God...and the God of peace.** The **peace of God** promises to keep you and the **God of peace** promises to stay with you. The **peace of God** is an overwhelming security that everything is okay in my relationship with God and with others. It is a feeling and a fact based on the undeserved forgiveness and patience of God. Those who experience God's peace in the midst of a heart-wrenching trial cannot explain it as it is something that defies comprehension... it passes all understanding. When God's peace overwhelms my heart sometimes I just want to sing in praise to God. (He doesn't mind my old, raspy, singing voice.)

> "When life's burdens get so heavy and it seems I'm all alone,
>
> I cast my care on Jesus and come boldly to His throne.
>
> I find His grace sufficient when His promises I heed,
>
> For His very life He sacrificed and He lives to intercede.
>
> He is the Lord of lords, and when He speaks, winds and waves obey.
>
> When Jesus whispers, "Peace be still," then darkness turns to day,
>
> And as I'm trusting in my Savior's Word, doubts and fears all cease,
>
> And beneath the shelter of His wings, I'm at rest in perfect peace.
>
> <small>(Used by permission from The Wilds song book)</small>

Write out a verse or chorus of one of your favorite songs about God's peace.

_____
_____
_____
_____

2. Read Philippians 4:8 again. One more time. Got it? Philippians 4:8 is the classic passage that deals with improper thinking. Wrong thinking leads to wrong feelings which lead to wrong actions. When someone is discontent with God, they will probably wrestle with worry, fear, anger, bitterness, or impure thinking. God wants to help us with our thinking and gives us criteria for what we should think about. It seems so easy to be consumed with the negative, difficult, hardships of life that we forget about the positive, encouraging, blessings of God. In a normal day, would you say that you think about things that are true, honest, pure, and lovely or things that are deceitful, dishonest, impure, and crude? Which does TV dwell on? Which fits the conversations of many of your friends? Which way does what you read online or in text messages lean? To help you with these questions, match the following words and phrases.

TRUE / HONEST / JUST / PURE / LOVELY / ADMIRABLE / EXCELLENT / PRAISEWORTHY

- No secrets, no hidden agendas, no make-believe situations _____
- It is right _____
- Truthful, candid, straightforward, free from deceit or trickery _____
- Innocent, pure, blameless, free from defilement _____
- Good repute, well spoken of, reputable _____
- Dear to someone, beloved, acceptable, pleasing _____
- Virtuous, moral excellence, superior goodness _____
- Commendable, worshipful, awe-inspiring _____

Now think again about your favorite TV shows, your favorite Internet sites, and your conversations with your friends and see if they fit into God's criteria for proper thinking in Philippians 4:8. How did you do? What do you need to do to get your thinking in line with a Philippians 4:8 mind-set? How could proper thinking help you with your anger? Your worry? Your fears? Your lusts? Your discontented heart?

_____
_____

3. **Those things, which ye have both learned, and received, and heard, and seen in me, do: and the God of peace shall be with you.** The key to contagious joy is a contented heart. Since Paul had both the joy and the contented heart while he was chained to a soldier in prison, he obviously experienced God's peace and protection over his heart and mind. In what way do you need to change your thinking to match Paul's?

- Paul lived with a God-confidence (Philippians 1) _____
_____

- Paul lived with an unselfish attitude (Philippians 2) _____
_____

- Paul lived with an eternal focus (Philippians 3) _____
_____

- Paul lived with a contented heart (Philippians 4) _____
_____

"Lord, let Your peace guard and keep my heart. Thank You. Amen."

WEEK 6: A CONTENTED HEART.

THURSDAY: PHILIPPIANS 4:10-13

CONTENTMENT COMES FROM AN UNDERSTANDING OF GOD'S POWER

But I rejoiced in the Lord greatly, that now at the last your care of me hath flourished again; wherein ye were also careful, but ye lacked opportunity. Not that I speak in respect of want: for I have learned, in whatsoever state I am, therewith to be content. I know both how to be abased, and I know how to abound: every where and in all things I am instructed both to be full and to be hungry, both to abound and to suffer need. I can do all things through Christ which strengtheneth me.

But I rejoiced in the Lord greatly, that now at the last your care (your concern) for **me has flourished again** (has been revived and renewed); **wherein ye were also careful, but ye lacked opportunity** (I fully understand that your hearts were full of care and concern for me but you did not have the chance to do anything about it). **Not that I speak in respect of want** (Please do not misunderstand me. I am not saying all of this because I need or want something from you): **for I have learned to be content in** whatever **state**, circumstances, or situations I happen to be in. **I know both how to be abased** (I know how to get along having nothing and I refuse to complain when those times come), **and I know how to abound** (I know how to respond in prosperity and I refuse to gloat or be wasteful when those times come): **every where and in all things** (in either of these situations) **I am instructed** (I have learned the secret) **both to be full** (to live with abundant prosperity) **and to be hungry** (to live with absolute poverty), **both to abound and to suffer need. I can do all things through Christ** who strengthens **me**.

1. Our world is bent on convincing us that we do not have enough money, things, or stuff. When we are in tune with "getting" but not with "giving," it will be evident in the way we work, we save, we give, and we play. There are two familiar verses in this section that have been a comfort and an encouragement to God's people for hundreds of years. Have you memorized Philippians 4:11 and 4:13? Take a minute and say both of them five times to yourself and get them locked into your mind. Describe the last time that God brought one of these verses to your mind and how it helped you to deal with whatever you were facing at that time.

_____

_____

_____

2. In context, Paul used these verses to describe how he viewed and handled life—both the good and the bad. In verse 12 he said, **I know both how to be abased** (to be in need), **and I know how to abound** (to have plenty)**: every where and in all things I am instructed both to be full and to be hungry, both to abound and to suffer need.** In other words, Paul did not base his joy on what he had or did not have. Whether he was hungry or well fed, he kept a smile on his face. His joy was not based on his personal comfort, the things that he had, or whether or not everybody liked him. He was content with his God and what his God had permitted into his life. What do you want that God has not already given you? In what way do you think God has been unfair to you? At what point will you be completely satisfied? When will you be able to be "thankful" for what God has given you rather than craving what He has not given? Are you

discontent? Has a discontented heart stolen your God-confidence, your unselfish attitude, or your eternal focus? It doesn't need to. Paul lived with contagious, outrageous joy and so can you! What does Exodus 20:17 command and warn us about?

_____

What words did Moses use in Exodus 20:17 to describe these thoughts?

• Are you satisfied with the home you live in?_____

• Are you content with your wife? _____

• Are you satisfied with the comforts that make life easier?_____

• Are you content with your car or truck? _____

• Are you content with what God has already given you? _____

3. Covetousness is the enemy of contentment. A discontented heart results in a morbid life devoid of all joy. Meditate on the verses below and ask yourself the four questions that follow. Honestly weigh each question in your heart before God.

• **And He said unto them, Take heed, and beware of covetousness: for a man's life consisteth not in the abundance of the things which he possesseth** (Luke 12:15).

• **Let your conversation be without covetousness; and be content with such things as ye have: for He hath said, I will never leave thee, nor forsake thee. So that we may boldly say, The Lord is my helper, and I will not fear what man shall do unto me** (Hebrews 13:5-6).

What do you want that God has not already given you?
_____

In what way do you think God has been unfair to you?
_____

At what point will you be completely satisfied?
_____

When will you be able to be "thankful" for what God has given you rather than craving more and more?
_____
_____

4. **I can do all things through Christ which strengtheneth me.** The power, strength, and enablement that God offers is (sad to say) not often taken advantage of. This verse is not to be used as a mystical rabbit's foot that can make us faster than a speeding bullet or able to leap tall buildings with a single bound, but to give us the assurance that we CAN be content in a discontented, covetous world. I can't in my own strength. I can in the power and strength that God gives. What area of your life are you currently discontent with and think things will never change or turn out for the best? What does Philippians 4:13 say to you?

_____
_____

"Lord, forgive me for my covetous attitude and discontented heart. I can be content. I can be thankful for both the good and bad in life. I can by Your strength. Thank You, Lord."

Week 6: A contented heart.
Friday: Philippians 4:14-23

Contentment comes from an understanding of God's provision

Notwithstanding ye have well done, that ye did communicate with my affliction. Now ye Philippians know also, that in the beginning of the gospel, when I departed from Macedonia, no church communicated with me as concerning giving and receiving, but ye only. For even in Thessalonica ye sent once and again unto my necessity. Not because I desire a gift: but I desire fruit that may abound to your account. But I have all, and abound: I am full, having received of Epaphroditus the things which were sent from you, an odor of a sweet smell, a sacrifice acceptable, well pleasing to God. But my God shall supply all your need according to His riches in glory by Christ Jesus. Now unto God and our Father be glory for ever and ever. Amen. Salute every saint in Christ Jesus. The brethren which are with me greet you. All the saints salute you, chiefly they that are of Caesar's household. The grace of our Lord Jesus Christ be with you all. Amen.

Notwithstanding (nevertheless) **ye have well done, that ye did communicate with my affliction** (it was good of you to share in my need and troubles). **Now ye Philippians know also, that in the beginning of the gospel** (in the early days of serving together), **when I departed from Macedonia, no church communicated with me as concerning giving and receiving, but ye only** (you guys kept me financially alive). **For even in Thessalonica ye sent once and again unto my necessity.** (Even when I was helping others, time and time again you took care of my needs. You are the most giving friends I have in the ministry.) **Not because I desire a gift: but I desire fruit that may abound to your account** (it's not really about the money you send me, but the way God has and will bless you because you give so willingly). **But I have all, and abound: I am full** (I'm good! I have more than I need and certainly more than I deserve), **having received of Epaphroditus the things which were sent from you, an odor of a sweet smell, a sacrifice acceptable, well pleasing to God.** (Don't think I can't see that this is a sacrifice from you. You are definitely helping me but your sacrifice does not go unnoticed by God. He is well pleased with your giving hearts.) **But my God shall supply all your need according to His riches in glory by Christ Jesus.** (Some of you have given so much, you have given out of your own need. I promise you on what I know of our great God. He will take care of your every need. He can and He will.)

1. Well, we've made it to the end of our study of Paul's encouraging, joy-producing letter to the Philippians. These last ten verses almost sound like a "Thank You" note. Who has recently encouraged your heart but you have not yet thanked? Write three names of individuals that you will e-mail, text, or write a quick note of thanks to.

___

2. Paul thanked the Philippians for their generous giving to other believers in need. God uses people (like you and me) to supply the needs of others. Do you tithe? Do you consistently give to your church, missions, camps, schools, and other ministries that seek to reach people for Christ? There are many in need. There are also many who think that they cannot afford to give to those in need. Write out Philippians 4:19 on the next page. This verse is a comfort to both those in need and those who should give to those in need.

3. Old Testament writers referred to God as "Jehovah-jireh" which means, God will provide. God knows what we need. We sometimes think we need what we want. What if God gave us everything we wanted and not what we needed? While we may concentrate on what would give us temporal happiness, God knows what will give us eternal joy. As we learned yesterday, there is a constant battle raging between contentment and covetousness. List two things that you need but God has not given you and then meditate on how "not having" those things could help you depend on God more, and yourself less. Have fun meditating.

4. Paul is saying in verses 20-23, "I need to say good-bye." He is emphasizing in his final words the importance of Christian friendship, Christian accountability, Christian encouragement, and Christian unity. If we are going to successfully (and joyfully) fight the world, the flesh, and the devil, we had better not waste too much time in fighting each other. True joy comes from being right with God and right with others. Is there anyone you can think of that you cannot talk to? Is there anyone you are so upset with you would never willingly shake their hand, give a hug, or wish them well? Remember, an understanding of God's people, God's presence, God's peace, God's power, and God's provision is the key to real joy--outrageous, contagious joy.

Now unto God and our Father be glory for ever and ever. Amen. (Keep your focus on glorifying our loving, heavenly Father.) **Salute every saint in Christ Jesus.** (Say "Hey" to all my believing friends. By the way, that is every believer. Euodias! Syntyche! You should be able to give each other a hug…at least shake hands and say "hey" or "howdy" to each other.) **The brethren which are with me greet you. All the saints salute you, chiefly they that are of Caesar's household.** (All of your friends with me here in my house arrest and all of the secret believers in the palace also say "Hi.") **The grace** (both the power and the desire to please God) **of our Lord Jesus Christ be with you all. Amen.**

What thoughts about your God or your friends do you need God's grace to help you change so you too can experience God's gift of outrageous, contagious joy?

"Lord, You've taught me much about real joy from Your Word. Your grace will enable me to experience outrageous, contagious joy as I live with a God-confidence, an unselfish attitude, an eternal focus, and a contented heart. Thank You, Lord."

Saturday & Sunday
Review

Philippians 4:1-23

What did Philippians 4:1-3 teach you about God's people, a contented heart, and contagious joy?

_____
_____
_____
_____
_____
_____
_____
_____
_____
_____

What did Philippians 4:4-6 teach you about God's presence, a contented heart, and contagious joy?

_____
_____
_____
_____
_____
_____
_____
_____
_____
_____

What did Philippians 4:7-9 teach you about God's peace, a contented heart, and contagious joy?

_____
_____
_____
_____
_____
_____
_____
_____

What did Philippians 4:10-13 teach you about God's power, a contented heart, and contagious joy?

_____
_____
_____
_____
_____
_____
_____
_____

What did Philippians 4:14-23 teach you about God's provision, a contented heart, and contagious joy?

_____
_____
_____
_____
_____
_____
_____
_____

The Secret of Outrageous, Contagious Joy

Principle One: Philippians 1:1-30

A God-confidence produces sustaining joy!

Principle Two: Philippians 2:1-30

An unselfish spirit produces unspeakable joy!

Principle Three: Philippians 3:1-21

An eternal focus produces outrageous joy!

Principle Four: Philippians 4:1-23

A contented heart produces contagious joy!